RENDING THE VEIL

RENDING THE VEIL

THE MYSTICISM OF THE GOSPEL OF PHILIP

WARD J. BAUMAN

Foreword by Cynthia Bourgeault

BOOK PUBLISHING COMPANY
RHINEBECK, NEW YORK

Quotations from the Bible are sometimes my own translations, and at other times taken from *The Inclusive Bible: The First Egalitarian Translation* (Sheed and Ward, 2009).

Paperback ISBN 9781966608233
eBook ISBN 9781966608240

Library of Congress Cataloging-in-Publication Data

Names: Bauman, Ward J. author
Title: Rending the veil : the mysticism of the Gospel of Philip / Ward J. Bauman ; forward by Cynthia Bourgeault.
Other titles: Gospel of Philip. English
Description: Rhinebeck, New York : Monkfish Book Publishing Company, [2026]
Identifiers: LCCN 2026001308 (print) | LCCN 2026001309 (ebook) | ISBN 9781966608233 paperback | ISBN 9781966608240 ebook
Subjects: LCSH: Gospel of Philip--Criticism, interpretation, etc. | Gnosticism | Mysticism
Classification: LCC BS2860.P67 B38 2026 (print) | LCC BS2860.P67 (ebook)
LC record available at https://lccn.loc.gov/2026001308
LC ebook record available at https://lccn.loc.gov/2026001309

Book and cover design by Colin Rolfe

Monkfish Book Publishing Company
22 East Market Street, Suite 304
Rhinebeck, New York 12572
(845) 876-4861
monkfishpublishing.com

to

all who

long for transcendence

CONTENTS

FOREWORD

It is my honor and pleasure to introduce you to my longtime friend and colleague Ward Bauman. For those who have long known Ward as a skillful and generous spiritual guide, this book brings forward yet another of his multifaceted talents, this time in the field of biblical scholarship.

I consider Ward to be an *amateur* scholar in the higher sense of the word, which means a *lover*. In this present era of uber-professionalism, "amateur" may give the impression of being "less trained" or "less qualified." This is a pity, a blind spot of our own accreditation-obsessed times. *All* the great scholars, integral thinkers, and philosophers of our Western tradition are ultimately amateur scholars—that is, if they have anything to say at all—because integral thinking is by definition cross-disciplinary and trans-rational, drawing on bandwidths of knowing that go deeper than mere intellectual manipulation. In the finest sense of the tradition, an amateur scholar is one who dives into a subject for the sheer love of it and allows this love to light the way to genuine integral insight. An amateur scholar may (or may not) hold a PhD; he or she may or may not be up to date on the latest critical research methods or scholarly controversies dominating the field. But these deficits (if that's what they are) are dependably more than compensated for by a freshness of approach and often boldness of insight that tends to get bred out of a would-be scholar in the course of their professional training (been there, done that!).

You will see those integrative qualities working overtime in Ward's brilliant re-imagining of the Gospel of Philip laid before us in this remarkable new commentary, truly a labor of love.

Ward has loved the Gospel of Philip for as long as I have known him, nearly three decades now. Back in the early 2000s, when he was just settling into his new post as director of the Episcopal House of Prayer at St John's Abbey in Collegeville, Minnesota, popular editions of the so-called "gnostic gospels" were just beginning to make their way into the hands of the general public, driven in significant part by Elaine Pagel's groundbreaking 1979 bestseller of that same title, the first book to call popular attention to a treasure trove of extra-biblical New Testament scriptures that had been accidentally discovered in an urn in the upper Egyptian desert in 1945. The forty-six manuscripts comprising this collection were a mostly mixed bag of early Christian wisdom teachings commonly understood to have emerged directly from Jesus, passed down via his early (mostly second and third century) disciples. For scholars and practitioners alike, this sudden infusion of invigorating and challenging new wisdom material functioned pretty much like catnip; suddenly every Tom, Dick, and Harry was on the scent! The main channel of scholarship steered overwhelmingly toward the Gospel of Thomas, arguably the most important text in the collection. Ward Bauman headed like a bee to honey toward the Gospel of Philip. His loyalty to this text has remained unflagging for all these two decades, and like all faithful and committed love journeys, it has yielded rich results.

The Gospel of Philip, one of the slimmer and more obviously "gnostic" in the collection, is challenging in significant ways. The subject matter is itself high-voltage: an unflinching exploration of the relationship between spiritual and sexual union; between love at the highest degrees of spiritual consummation and what this text proclaims to be its most powerful sacramental analogue: human conjugal love rightly understood and enacted.

This is not a message for the faint of heart, even in our own times. The inroads of more than two thousand years of puritanical and shame-based moral teachings have done their work, to be sure, leaving one trembling and oftentimes with head spinning to navigate a way through this small wisdom text that future, less reactive generations, might be less reticent to identify as the metaphysical charter of Christian tantra.

Add to this the fact that the text has a complicated and fraught textual history. In its original manuscript presentation, it lacks clear internal divisions recognizable as chapters, topics, or even pericopes. This is not unusual in ancient manuscripts; in almost all modern editions (including the Bible) page numbers, line numbers, and headings are purely editorial conventions. But the Gospel of Philip has clearly undergone a much more dramatic and intentional structural rearrangement over the centuries, either to clarify or further obfuscate its sensitive subject matter. Even a cursory comparison of the several contemporary versions available reveals wide discrepancies in sequencing, intelligibility, and overall angle of approach—i.e., even more than usual at the whim of scholarly attempts to impose order and coherence on an unruly text.

Ward Bauman wades into this morass bravely, bringing the best of his critical discernment skills to the table, augmented by his own deep contemplative insight and an unflagging confidence in the coherence of the message being proclaimed in this text. Such contemplative insight is most reliably grown through years of faithful time logged on the mediation cushion. As it stabilizes, it confers a growing capacity to "recognize like by like," one of the cornerstones of the hermetic and alchemical paths.

In the light of his own well-developed capacity here, Ward is able to recognize that the author of this gospel is spiritually sophisticated, well-trained in subtle discernment, and entirely capable of imagining and successfully orchestrating a complex metaphysical conceit cloaked in the garments of late Judaic Temple Mysticism, but now seamlessly transposed to a Christian sacramental milieu. In other words, that he or she is a Wisdom teacher in the finest sense of the term. And even while scholars throw up their hands at the disorder of the manuscript, they acknowledge the brilliance of some of its aphorisms and its full continuity with the apodictic and paradigm-busting language of the Wisdom pedagogical breed. Through his own deep familiarity with the Wisdom genre, Ward is able to make the imaginative leaps and fill in the gaps—correctly, I believe.

While this new commentary acknowledges and makes skillful use of primary critical research tools, it is ultimately Ward's own well-seasoned contemplative insight that guides his hand as he slowly discerns a pattern beneath the surface chaos: the slow and strategic unfoldment of five progressive stages as one makes one's way along the path of conscious love (sometimes called the "Fifth way" path), based on an increasingly subtle penetration into the "holy of holies" of the Temple metaphor: from the outer porches to the inner sanctum; from purification, through baptism, anointing and eucharist, into the mystical bridal chamber and out again into the world; bearing both the fragrance and the mystical kerygma of the Great Restoration, the final consummation of love. The overarching framework, once discerned, invites a natural regrouping of the chapters and allows one to read this text as a coherent and strategic allegory for progression along this inward path of the heart.

See what you think as you taste this coherence for yourself. If nothing else, I believe that Ward Bauman's *Rending the Veil: The Mysticism of the Gospel of Philip* is both the boldest of the interpretive commentaries now available, and most respectful of the text's ultimate intelligence: its ultimate ability to reveal its secrets to those with "eyes to see and ears to hear."

The Rev. Cynthia Bourgeault, PhD
Writer, retreat leader, amateur scholar

GENERAL INTRODUCTION

How many of us know what it would mean to be a fully realized human being, that is, a person reaching their highest anthropic potential? How many have heard us compared to amphibious creatures, in that we're to live fully in the spiritual realm as well as the physical? Like fish swimming in the ocean looking for water, we spend our lives futilely looking for God, with whom we already live, move, and have our being. Instead, we seem content to remain, as it were, tadpoles, living and dying undeveloped, missing the ecstatic experience of knowing the freedom of being a fully developed child of God.

Philip also describes the human condition as slavery. "A slave," Philip says, "longs for freedom" (The Gospel of Philip 5:15). The human predicament is that we don't even know we are enslaved; we're simply unhappy and restless and don't know why. We are stuck in our early stage of development and it is unpleasant. We can't escape, so we act out or try to compensate by self-aggrandizement. It isn't working. The world is in a mess because most everyone are enslaved in one way or another. Philip shows us how to change, to evolve and transform into our highest potential, transcending our present condition.

In time, we live limited lives, and old age and death come way too soon. But in the spiritual realm, we're freed to a timeless vision and experience. We discover that our small, limited ego is connected to time, but our true essential self is not. But when we become truly amphibious, we are freed from the constructs of society, discovering that we're in "the great age of the eternal now," as Philip puts it (4:15). We are already in God's reign, and it is glorious. Now united with God we fulfill the role of God's own by entering the transcendental imaginal realm and bringing truth, beauty, and goodness into this earthly domain. We've become beings of light in earthly garments.

These are just two of the ways in which I believe the Gospel of Philip is a Christian mystical primer intended to initiate those who are ready into dynamic secrets.

THE COMMUNITY OF THE GOSPEL OF PHILIP

My sources include the work of several scholars, most importantly the German Wilhelm Schneemelcher, editor of *New Testament Apocrypha*, who believes the Gospel of Philip dates to the second century.[1] It was used by the Valentinians, according to the fourth-century Christian apologist Epiphanius (315-403 CE) in his work, *Refutation of All the Heresies*. These were a group of gnostic Christians who followed their spiritual leader, Valentinus (101-160 CE). And if Epiphanius' claim is correct, this would place it, or an early compilation of it, clearly in the second century.

It is unlikely that Valentinus authored the Gospel of Philip, as some have supposed. We know little of him except that he came from the region of Egypt to Rome, where he came close to being elected its bishop. The Valentinians—those

---

[1] Wilhelm Schneemelcher, R. Mcl. Wilson, trans., *New Testament Apocrypha, Vol. 1: Gospels and Related Writings* (Westminster/John Knox Press, 1991), The Gospel of Philip, 183.

who looked to Valentinus as their leader—were a large and accepted arm of the early Christian movement.

Epiphanius' claims against the Valentinians, whom he called Borborites, or "filthy ones," are spurious at best. He promoted conspiracy theories that their rites included sexual orgies, and that they ate infants and drank menstrual blood in their rituals. But there is no other evidence, from their writings or history to support such horrendous accusations. Nor were they even Gnostic in the sense that Epiphanius understood it. He was eager to make all groups which did not conform to his form of Christian orthodoxy heretical, resorting to rumors and slander. (Similar accusations were later levied against the Jews in their rites. We know the hatred and violence this engendered in the Christian populace. Which should be a warning for all of us to step back and listen, learn and trust the sources themselves, and not so much what others claim about them.) This likely is one reason for the disassembly of the text of the Gospel of Philip, hiding it from those who would misuse and misunderstand it. My work has been an attempt to correct this bias against an ancient, sacred text.

Though we do not know the authorship, we can deduct from the text itself that it was written by early Jewish-Christian mystics who had experienced the secret teachings passed on by Jesus to his disciples. The Gospel of Mark even speaks of secret teachings that Jesus gave to his disciples that were not made public (Mark 4:11).

Philip tells us that Jesus "took everyone by surprise, for he did not reveal himself as he truly was, but only according to the capacities of those who were able to perceive him" (3:9). The Gospel of Thomas echoes this, as well. Jesus said, "I disclose my mysteries to those ready for Mystery."[2] And in

[2] Lynn C. Bauman, Ward J. Bauman, Cynthia Bourgeault, *The Luminous Gospels: Thomas, Mary Magdalene, and Philip* (Praxis Publishing, 2008),

a dialogue between Peter and Mary Magdalene recorded in the Gospel of Mary Magdalene, Peter implies that Jesus gave private teachings to his disciples as they were ready: "Sister, we know that the Savior greatly loved you above all other women, so tell us what you remember of his words that we ourselves do not know or perhaps have never heard."[3] Thomas also states that Jesus' "secret sayings I have written down."[4] All three gospels: Thomas, Mary, and Philip claim to be based on Jesus' "secret sayings."

This gospel was written long before there was an established Christian religion, or the major councils of the Church or authorized sacred texts. These Jewish followers of Jesus left a blueprint, as they understood it, for human transformation, according to their experience. It's an internal path which everyone can make when ready to the ground of their being. The basic teaching has to do with temple mysticism, discovering the Holy Spirit, the *Shekinah*, the Divine Presence dwelling at our core, which becomes revelatory. Everything, according to Philip, is an incarnation (2:26). This gospel was an initiation into this enlightening experience.

This Gospel was originally treasured and kept secret to all but a select few. Those who were invited in were those who had been chosen and initiated into its mysteries. At some point—we don't know when—it appears to have been disordered, or "rent asunder."[5] This intentional disordering was possibly meant to hide its contents and protect its teachings from those who were unprepared and would not understand the hidden mysteries. This is an assumption but

---

The Gospel of Thomas, 62, 28.

[3] The Dialogues of Mary Magdalene, 67.

[4] The Gospel of Thomas, 1, 9.

[5] Schneemelcher, *New Testament Apocrypha, Vol. 1*, 184.

seems to bear out as we delve into the text. (More on this in a minute.)

If used, apart from the oversight of an appropriate teacher, the chances of misunderstanding the Gospel of Philip were deemed too great. To guard their safety and the potential misuse, these teachings were kept secret until it was discerned an initiate was prepared.

> This truth is important and its excellence strengthens us to go inward through the symbols, humble and often rejected though they may be, and by this lowly means to enter into the presence of the fullness of glory—glory upon glory, light upon light, power upon power. Those who have reached this perfection open the way into the truth of hidden things for the rest of us, and thus saints and sacred beings bring us to the threshold . . . and invite us within (1:7).

ITS RECENT DISCOVERY

Thus, the Gospel of Philip was discovered buried with other ancient books in 1945 near the village of Nag Hammadi in Egypt. What was found, and later understood, was a library of books from a monastery established by St. Pachomius in the fourth century. We are not sure why this library was buried, but because the books were carefully preserved in a clay jar, it is assumed that they were treasured and loved. In all likelihood the books were buried because Archbishop Athanasius of Alexandria sent a letter in 367 CE to Egyptian monasteries listing the books he deemed orthodox and urging the monasteries to purge their libraries of all others.

We can assume, therefore, that this monastery at least felt it must comply, but the monks, or some of the monks, could not bear to destroy treasured though unorthodox texts. They hid them in the desert close to their monastery, hoping to dig them up when it was safe and acceptable to do so.

This library remained buried until 1945 when a poor farmer, digging in his fields, found them and dug them up. Although not considered orthodox even today, these texts are treasured, giving us a window into early Christian writings before the formation of the councils of the Church, where they chose by ballot what was and was not considered orthodox—that is, "correct" belief. By contrast, these earlier Christians emphasized correct *practice*. The Gospel of Philip is a text about orthopraxis.

It should also be stated that after the Church councils, when orthodox belief was defined in the fourth century, a third of the extant churches worldwide eventually were declared heretical. This included the churches of the East, Syria through to China and India, as well as the churches of North Africa, including Egypt and Ethiopia. After the canons of the Christian Bible were formally fixed in 382 CE, following the dictates set by Athanasias at the earlier council of Alexandria, other texts, with a divergent understanding of Christianity, were declared heretical, and consequently often banned from usage.

I use the term "imperial Christianity" throughout this book. I am referencing the Christianity that came into existence when Emperors Constantine and later Theodosius made Christianity the religion of the state. Under Constantine, the emperor became head of both church and state. With this came the effort to unify the Christian faith 350 years after Jesus' ministry. The councils of the Church during the fourth century sought to find a singular understanding of Jesus and his message, with the power of the empire to enforce the results. What was almost lost in the effort was the inner path that Jesus gave us.

But remnants of Jesus' authentic teachings continued on in the more distant monasteries, especially in the churches of the East. The imperial Church became a belief system that externalized God by objectifying God.

The Nicene Creed was adopted in 381 CE, and began to be inserted into the Eucharistic celebration to control and inhibit those in disagreement from participation in the rite. The phrase concerning Jesus' singularity as "the only Son of God, eternally begotten of the Father" was particularly aimed at Christians who claimed that all people are children of God, and "siblings" of Jesus (4:28). With this also came the use of excommunication as a means of enforcing the newly formed orthodoxy.

This orthodoxy was turned not only against Christians who differed in respect to belief and practice but began to fall heavily upon the non-Christian populace, especially Jewish populations in disproportionate numbers. Various forms of the Inquisition later became a cruel and evil means of forcing both Jewish and Muslim citizens to submit to the Christian faith or be expelled from "Christian lands." Christian armies in the West also took up war against Islam as well as the Christian Greek-speaking East in multiple crusades. Jesus' clear declarations that his "realm is not of this world," and the sword is not a means to bring it about (John 18:36), were disregarded in favor of a Christian state with the power to subjugate its populace by force. This eventually even carried over into the non-Christian world as Christian missionaries followed the Christian armies in subjugating native populations worldwide. In the effort to impose their own beliefs upon native peoples, there was little attempt to understand their inherent knowledge and wisdom.

MEANING FOR TODAY

By publishing the Gospel of Philip now, I'm not trying to promote a new orthodoxy or belief system, but am rather seeking to reveal an alternative form of the Jesus movement that was deemed important and authentic in ancient days. I believe that it is valuable for us to see what this important branch of early Christians understood Jesus and his message and his particular path of salvation.

The inner path frees us from focusing on controversial or divergent forms of belief while offering the path that transcends those beliefs. It also offers us a path to direct knowledge of God, rather than objectifying God through descriptions and creeds, telling us what to believe about God and the person of Jesus Christ. Christian orthodoxy required one to believe the Christian myths and doctrines in order to be a true Christian. For the Philip-Christians, the deeper application of Jesus' teachings was the means to salvation, not what one believed about Jesus. Belief came after one had experienced the "truth of hidden things" (1:7). "Those who gain wisdom from truth are liberated beings" (3:29).

In this book I am rather boldly making a historical assumption (though based on scholarship) that Jesus existed, that his ministry took place, and was documented years after his departure. I am not interested here in proving that he was crucified, nor that he rose from the dead. I am not addressing the miracles or the other gospel (canonical) stories of his life and ministry.

I am letting the Gospel of Philip define what Jesus' crucifixion and resurrection meant at that time through its writings. It is essential to allow this early community of Jewish Christians to interpret those experiences from their own understanding. They teach that Jesus continued to live on spiritually after his death and resurrection (in whatever form it may have taken), and his spiritual energy continued to engage later generations. Philip teaches that the Spirit of Christ is spread over the earth both within nature and within humanity, and is the dynamic conscious energy that moves in and through "all the many things." Philip's assumption is, as Jesus told his followers (as recorded also in the Gospel of John 14:16-17): "I will ask the One who sent me to give you another helper to be with you always—the Spirit of Truth, whom the world cannot accept since the world neither sees her nor recognizes her; but you can recognize the Spirit because she remains with you and will be within you."

I am aware that what I'm presenting will be called heretical and even blasphemous. However, I think it is a worthwhile investigation to revisit these ancient texts to discover for ourselves the truth of this ancient esoteric Christian path. We should ask ourselves, *What was the Spirit teaching these ancient Christians?* In fact, perhaps it's time to eliminate "heresy" from our vocabulary in order to hear anew what the Spirit of God has to say.

I am only presenting what I've understood with the caveat that I too have prejudices and cultural chains. I am looking at this text through my own vocabulary and ideas, which are not the language of this ancient book. I use psychological concepts and theological language that was unavailable to ancient Christians. For example, I use the term "ego" in identifying that part of ourselves we might identify as the self, but which is yet not spiritually transformed through spiritual work. Philip wouldn't use such a term yet does speak of "the true self" as opposed to the self prior to a rebirth in God, which comes close to what I might refer to as the ego-self.

I also use the term "evolution," in speaking of spiritual transformation. Of course, this is a modern term, but the concept of human transformation is common to Philip, which seems close to my understanding of the evolutionary forces at work in human transformation. What is unique here is that this evolutionary or transformative force only takes place when my soul finds unity with God's presence within me. So although my language and ideas are recent, my hope is that they will awaken within many a new sense of possibility and the ongoing revelation that is within a relationship with a God humans can't fully define.

PHILIP'S MYSTICAL LINEAGE

Remember that many of our mystics in Western Christianity were also declared heretical, even at times to the point of death. I am not afraid of being called heretical, as my own search has been predicated upon a trust in the Holy Spirit within me. Also, I do not make the claim that what is being taught us from this ancient community is always my own settled belief. I come at this with openness to the Spirit within to lead and guide without an authoritative theological stance. That said, much of what I hear in Philip finds echoes in the mystics who also investigated the Gospel through their own experience and speak of what they heard and experienced.

I bring this text into dialogue with other mystics, first with Jewish mysticism as expressed by second-century Christian Jews, and then with Christian mystics from both East and West. I compare Philip to some of the Hebrew Scriptures. I also reference the mysticism of St. Paul. Paul says, "You died, and your life is hidden with Christ in God. But when Christ—who is your life—is revealed, you too will be revealed with Christ in Glory" (Colossians 3:3). And "We are heirs of God and co-heirs with Christ, sharing in Christ's suffering and sharing in Christ's glory" (Ephesians 8:17). The mystics who claim to be heirs of Philip tell us that we too are to become one with God and thus heirs with Christ, indeed becoming Christ. "If you say, 'I am the Christ,' it will indeed cause a reaction. May it be that I receive whatever is needed to withstand in the cosmos when that is uttered!" (2:11)

I've also chosen two mystics from the Church of the East: Isaac the Syrian, a desert hermit in the eighth century, who was a prolific writer in Syriac and came from the land where the Gospel of Philip likely emerged; and Symeon the New Theologian, an Eastern Orthodox monk of the tenth century who also wrote extensively of his mystical experiences. And then there's Meister Eckhart, a German from the fourteenth century, considered the most non-dual mystic of Western Christendom, who in my view has much in common with Philip.

When seen and understood within the context of a lineage, we are better able to understand the content and language of this gospel. I see Philip as among the earliest works we have of Christian mysticism. And glimmers of an emerging apophatic theology.

And I compare the Gospel of Philip to two other gospels which were discovered in Egypt in 1945: the Gospel of Thomas and the Gospel of Mary Magdalene. They, with Philip, were also rejected and declared heretical by the imperial Church. They are also of early composition and use similar language and images, and are thus compatible and helpful in interpreting Philip. Of particular interest is the fact that Philip was found bound together in the same codex with Thomas, a book of Jesus' sayings. We don't know the exact significance of this, but we might deduce that this was an ancient way of using the texts, having a gospel of the sayings of Jesus combined with a gospel applying those teachings.

The imperial Church eschewed the inner journey where we become united with God and find our inner authority, seeing as God sees. The Western Church especially objectifies God by approaching God from the outside theologically, seeking to find proofs for God. Philip, on the other hand, shows how to see from the inside out—seeing the world and ourselves as God sees us. Seeing through the eyes of God, grounded in the heart of God.

For the imperial Church, the baptismal rite was the means of salvation and thus an end in itself. In the Gospel of Philip, salvation is understood as unity with God, which can be discovered through the rite of baptism, but baptism isn't the end goal, only a starting point, leading us into a life-long relationship with God.

Philip understands scripture to be metaphorical, pointing to a deeper knowledge beyond the literal meaning of the words. For example, the virgin birth of Jesus by Mary is taken literally by the imperial Church, whereas Philip understands virginity as metaphorical of a pure spiritual state of being. We are to discover the deeper meaning of scripture, with the ears of the heart, where truth is really found. Jesus said, "What you hear with one ear, listen to with both, and then proclaim from the rooftop."[6]

The Gospel of Philip is not like the four canonical gospels of the New Testament in that it is not a story of Jesus and his teachings. It is instead a gospel in the sense that a

---

[6] The Gospel of Thomas, 33, 19.

community of early Christians wrote the text, as an interpretation of the Christian message, and its goal of salvation. There were many gospels written at that time, around the mid-second century, that also claimed a relationship with certain apostles. Most were written by those claiming a specific apostolic association. The Gospel of Philip does not claim a relationship with Philip other than the title and the fact that he is the only apostle mentioned in the text. This is not dissimilar from the Gospel of Matthew which also barely mentions Matthew and does not claim Matthew's authorship. These were likely written by a community who claimed a relationship with the work and teachings of the Apostles Matthew and Philip.

The Apostle Philip is said to have gone to the region of Greece and ultimately Syria doing mission work. In Syria he was martyred, and his tomb and basilica have been excavated there showing it was an ancient pilgrimage site. It can be assumed, therefore, that this community of Christians considered themselves spiritual heirs of the Apostle Philip.

The text was discovered in Egypt in a Coptic translation. But within the text, certain Greek and Syriac words were retained in the Coptic translation—words that would have been known to educated monks. Since Syriac words were in the original, Philip was likely originally written in Syriac by a Christian sect there before the mid-second century.[7] And since Greek was the language of the educated, it is also possible that it was written in Greek with Syriac words included, or in Syriac with Greek words included. Unfortunately, we don't have any original texts, only the Coptic translation.

Complicating this Coptic translation is the fact that the book appears scrambled or disordered in some way. This is the

[7] Syriac is a dialect of Aramaic, the language of Jesus and his apostles.

"intentional disordering" that we mentioned above. There are actually no paragraph separations, nor are there connections made between changes of thought. It is one long single document without any indication of changes in topics, thus it is difficult to know how to translate this text to make sense of it. There are consistent topics, but they are not presented in any particular order. It jumps from one topic to the next without any connection or continuity of ideas.

We can say with certainty that this text was always a compilation of concepts, thus a *florilegium*, or anthology of ideas. Each translator therefore must make the decision as to where paragraph separations and punctuations take place. In the *Luminous Gospels: Thomas, Mary Magdalene, and Philip*, in which I, as a committee member, was involved in the translation, we made the hard decisions after many discussions.

Mention is made in the text that the teachings are only for those prepared and ready to receive the mysteries. The unprepared are incapable of grasping its teachings. There is also the implication that participation in the mysteries happens after a person has entered more fully into the human experience, likely in mid-life. Philip says, "It is from the unseen world that the mysteries of truth are revealed through the iconic images" (4:3). The "iconic images" in Philip are the Christian mysteries, which it gives as: Baptism, Anointing, Eucharist, Marriage, and the Great Restoration. These symbols, or "icons" as Philip calls them, are meant to open and lead us into a deeper spiritual experience of resurrection, restoration to fullness of being, unity of being, and rebirth. This involves an evolution of human consciousness. Without transcendent awareness we are incapable of such knowledge.

WHO WROTE IT

As to who wrote this, we really do not know. Some scholars believe it was a compilation of different writers. This is possible. However, there are specific themes and consistent terms used throughout, which leads me to believe there is too much coherence for it to have been written by multiple and disparate authors. And the language is heavy with metaphors and phrases particular to itself.

This leads me to believe that it was produced by a community of early Christians over time, and that it was likely compiled by its teacher(s). Within the text there are several times when an author speaks in the first-person singular. "This is what I affirm," they say at one point regarding the resurrection of the dead. At another point they caution, "May it be that I am not found in a domain between" the resurrection and this world—a place where decisions are no longer possible. And another time, they speak in the first person regarding the garden of paradise, "In this garden it was said—even to me—'You may not eat of this, but you cannot consume that, though you desire it.'" This links the creation myth with our imminent experience. We all live in that garden and are responding to its truths, whether conscious of it or not.

In all three places, the author or authors are speaking with authority regarding important but controversial issues. We cannot know who they are, but we can see the importance and the gravity with which they understood these teachings and their use. We are also made aware that other Christian communities were not in total agreement over many of the issues being discussed here. Christianity in the second century was scattered throughout the known world and was as diverse in its beliefs and practices as it has ever been.

We do know that this was written by a Jewish-Christian community. In several passages they mention Jewish identity. “In our early Jewish days, we remained orphaned, having only a mother, but when we became followers of the Anointed One, for our sakes the Father joined our Mother” (5:16). This might even indicate a first century text. These Jewish Christians now see themselves as having become a new humanity. They, in fact, will say at one point that unity with God creates a “new human race,” and a new identity. This is, of course, a part of their mysticism, for they view unity with God as the singular human transformative experience. The Philip-Christians are teaching that the Gospel is participation in God as revealed by Jesus. Rather than belief *in* Jesus being the essential concern, they teach that by partaking in Jesus’ life and teachings we too become the Christ. This knowledge is not a belief but rather an experience of transcendent truth.

IS IT GNOSTIC?

The Gospel of Philip has been declared by many scholars to be a Gnostic text. This word or label is often used rather loosely to lump together sects that were divergent in their views and practices but maintained some Greek philosophical language. The Christians of this text believed that knowledge (*gnosis*) of God was salvation, so in that sense, yes they are gnostics, but they are not Gnostics, in the sense of following Greek philosophy *per se*, even though they do use vocabulary coming from Greek thought at that time.

St. Paul also used this word “gnostic” in speaking of spiritual knowledge: “I work so that their hearts will be strengthened, so that they will be knit together in love, enriched with full assurance by their knowledge [gnosis] of the mystery of God—namely Christ—in whom every treasure of wisdom and knowledge [gnosis] is hidden," it says in Colossians 2:2-3. And the word is common outside of Christianity, as well. Sufis, for instance, often call themselves "gnostics" in the same way, teaching that a spiritual knowledge of God is the goal of our earthly experience.

Greek Gnosticism is famously anti-body, disparaging the physical realm as evil while teaching that only the spiritual realm is good. Many Gnostics denigrated the body and its passions. But not these Philip-gnostics—they believed that the body as well as the soul were sacred. As was the earth, which they regarded as a paradise if one only has the eyes to see such truth. So in the traditional Gnostic sense of the word, this is not a Gnostic text.

I have already said I believe this to be a book of initiation into the mysteries. I came to this conclusion because of the many times it speaks of mysteries, secrets, and guidance needed in making this spiritual quest. When studied over time I began to see that there is consistency in the spiritual work being presented. It is all about "the inner journey" because it is about going deep into one's own being where God, the Holy Spirit, is accessible, and where a union between the soul and God takes place. It is what we are made for, but it takes a spiritual awakening and a transformation of our being to accomplish.

REORDERING THE TEXT

Over time I became frustrated with the disorder of the text because I could see certain themes and passages that clearly belonged together. I was encouraged in this view by reading

Schneemelcher's *New Testament Apocrypha*, where he quotes another scholar saying that it appears that many of the disconnected portions "originally belonged together."[8] To study the Gospel of Philip carefully is to see that many of these apparently disconnected portions have greater clarity when connected. Not only that, but the text in this new configuration offers a process and a sequence of spiritual experiences in order to reach our fullness of being.

I began to sense that the text themes were likely originally organized around this sequence: Jesus gave us the mysteries by which we are transformed: baptism, anointing, eucharist, restoration to fullness of being, and the bridal chamber, and birth of God. Seeing these themes throughout the text, I kept reorganizing them to facilitate the teaching of these materials.

One day I made the decision to take the book apart, separating the clusters of ideas to reorganize them into a more meaningful and readable whole. Next, I set about restructuring the text into a somewhat coherent entity based on the sequence found within the text: the prologue, baptism and anointing, eucharist, the bridal chamber, and the great restoration (5:1). I kept at this work for about a year until it felt like a piece, which was readable and cohesive. It still isn't perfect, but it works in making sense of this mystical text. This is what I am presenting in *The Reordered Gospel of Philip* in Part One.

I am hoping and trusting that my intuition with this work proves helpful, and that I might have restored a coherent and genuine part of the original that has been lost to us. What is presented is something that emerged out of my active imagination as I worked and prayed and sought to

---

[8] Schneemelcher, *New Testament Apocrypha, Vol. 1*, 187.

bring what I was seeing to a modern reader and, hopefully, practitioner of these mysteries. This work is intended to be a practical guide penetrating into the core of the Christian mysteries which offer a path to human transformation and fullness. Its validity will be confirmed in its application.

COMMENTING ON THE TEXT

Next, I began writing reflections on the reordered text, laying out the process of initiation which I believe is taught here. There are many parts of this text where I am still not sure what was meant or originally intended. I often compare my sense of this with other interpreters and scholars.[9] Some interpretations are clear to me by comparing one text with another within the document: one theme echoing or enhancing the other. For instance, I advance the controversial idea that Jesus was the son of Mary and Joseph, not having a miraculous virgin birth. This seems clear by comparing different passages, though it is not stated as blatantly as I have just put it. It is, however, clearly implied throughout the document and strengthened by bringing together multiple texts.

I want to honor the secrecy of these teachings and protect them as cautioned by the original teachers. The content is and should be taught through personal initiation into the experience, not through the dissemination of content. In that regard, I have attempted to avoid explication of the ineffable mystical experiences suggested by the teachings. These are only known by way of genuine experience. I leave

[9] I have already mentioned the importance of the scholar Wilhelm Schneemelcher. I also want to mention the importance of Jean-Yves LeLoup and his translation of the Gospel of Philip (into French, with the English translation by Joseph Rowe), and commend his introduction (Inner Traditions, 2004). It is the best introduction to this Gospel that I've read, and it encouraged me in my own approach.

the guidance of this work to the experience of the reader as much as possible.

There are, of course, many approaches to such an examination of the Gospel of Philip. There are many attempts, for instance, to overlay a philosophical system upon the text, such as so-called Valentinian Gnostic teachings. However, much of what we know about the Valentinians come not from their writings but from their detractors who were prejudiced by a desire to label them heretics, and thus unworthy of being heard. Even as we examine this manuscript today, we find aspects that are not what these detractors claimed. In fact, much of its language and vocabulary is consonant with the common Christian literature of the time.

My approach is always to take this work without overlaying much else upon it, letting its language and vocabulary be authoritative as much as is possible. My prayer is that in presenting this work I will have opened the windows of our Christian understanding of Jesus and his teachings to old currents that bring fresh and new winds of understanding and insight.

PHILIP THE APOSTLE

As I mentioned at the outset, there were many gospels written around the mid-second century that claimed a relationship with one of Jesus' original apostles. The Gospel of Philip does not specifically claim a relationship with the Philip who knew Jesus. Still, it might be helpful to examine the experience of the Apostle Philip and what he passed on to his followers.

The earliest mention of Philip in the canonical gospels takes place in the Gospel of John. After John baptizes Jesus, he tells his own followers, one of whom was Philip, that he has seen Jesus baptized with the Holy Spirit, saying, "Now I have seen for myself and have testified that this is the Only Begotten of God." The text continues:

> The next day, John was by the Jordan again with two of his disciples. Seeing Jesus walk by, John said, "Look! There's the Lamb of God!" The two disciples heard what John said and followed Jesus. When Jesus turned around and noticed them following, he asked them, "What are you looking for?" They replied, "Rabbi where are you staying?" "Come and see," Jesus answered. So they went to see and spent the rest of the day with him. (John 1:24-39)

Whatever they discovered that day convinced them that this was indeed the Messiah they were looking for.

> The next day, after Jesus had decided to leave for Galilee, he met Philip [again] and said, "Follow me." Philip came from Bethsaida, the same town as Andrew and Peter. Philip sought out Nathanael and said to him, "We've found the One that Moses spoke of in the Law, the One about whom the prophets wrote: Jesus of Nazareth, begot of Mary and Joseph." "From Nazareth?" said Nathanael. "Can anything good come from Nazareth?"
>
> "Come and see." (John 1:43-46)

Philip had been a disciple of John the Baptist, but quickly and faithfully became a disciple of Jesus. It is interesting that he used the same phrase Jesus used in answer to the inquiry of Andrew and John: "Come and see." This is the pedagogical approach in the Gospel of Philip. It never asks the reader to believe on hearsay alone, but to get involved and see for oneself, to verify it to oneself. Truth, according to Philip, can only be known as one encounters it.

We can only wonder what happened when they spent that first day with Jesus. We only know that Philip saw for himself and invited his friends to do the same. It is through living truth that we come to know truth. "Come and see for yourself," likewise, is the primary theme of the Gospel of Philip. Truth can be discovered from an encounter with the living Christ and apprehended within the depths of one's own being.

We have no record that the Apostle Philip was present at Jesus' baptism, but he was clearly influenced and taught by it, and saw it as a pivotal moment in Jesus' life and teaching. Philip would have also gone through John's baptism, as Jesus did. This community passed on the knowledge of Jesus' baptism as an exemplary experience for all humanity. It was there "he was restored to fullness of being." This is Jesus' visional moment, a personal awakening to the truth of his own essential self, his enlightenment. Humanity's fullness of being is its evolutionary trajectory, and a mystery into which Jesus initiated his disciples. For Philip—both the original apostle and the Gospel later written in his name—our physical baptisms are allegory, iconic truths pointing toward and leading us into our own resurrection and fullness of being.

Another significant inquiry of Jesus by the Apostle Philip took place at the Last Supper. As the canonical gospel says, Jesus was explaining his relationship with Abba God, Philip interrupted and said: "Rabbi, show us Abba God, and that will be enough for us."

> Jesus replied, "Have I been with you all this time, Philip, and still you don't know me?
>
> Whoever has seen me has seen Abba God. How can you say, 'Show us your Abba'? Don't you believe that I am in Abba God and God is in me? The words I speak are not spoken of myself, it is Abba God, living in me, who is accomplishing the works of God. Believe me that I am in God and God is in me, or else believe because of the works I do.'" (John 14:8-11)

Once again, Jesus invited Philip to know the truth by what he verified for himself. This is an intuitive knowing of the heart—sapiential knowledge. "The Father lives in the Son and the Son lives in the Father. This, then, is the Realm of the Heavens," states the Gospel of Philip (2:12). Clearly echoing the Apostle Philip's exchange with Jesus.

Another theme of the Gospel of Philip is "what you see from beyond comes because you yourself are transcending towards them" (3:4). In other words, truth is discovered as we are made capable of discerning it, evolving new and greater perceptivity. "Grace flows from his mouth—the source of the Logos, which also nourishes us in order that we might become complete" (4:10). Students of this ancient text are invited to know these truths from heart-knowing, while prayerfully encountering the source of the Logos within.

Our universe is understood by the ancient Christian community that produced the Gospel of Philip to be *theophanic*, filled with the Presence of God. Most of us are ignorant of this, even though it is a knowledge meant to be our birthright. Everything, according to Philip, arises through some form of incarnation. Everything is a bearer of divine life and meant to express that life in its own way. Humans who come awake to this reality seek this truth in everything, looking to find God in all forms of creation, in every human being. We cannot contain God, nor can we define God, but according to Philip, we can come to know this ineffable God in creation itself. And in knowing God we find our freedom and then help "the many things" to find theirs as well—to be their own essential self, imaging their Creator.

Imperial Christianity became a religion that kept many on the periphery of life, never going deep enough to know life's true reality, never having an experiential knowledge of truth. With Philip's message, these truths can be examined to discover for ourselves how to become a fully realized human being. Philip encourages us to go deep within, finding our essential nature. Philip invites us to understand ourselves as temples of the living God, and bearers of God's presence. Religion isn't something we identify with, by maintaining an elite set of beliefs, but something we become as we attain fullness of being.

Often our religious traditions have not helped us to "come and see" for ourselves but have rather kept us outside objectifying God and dependent upon the authority of others. But the Gospel of Philip, following the teachings of the Master, invites us into the inner chambers of our own being where truth is to be found and our sovereignty gained.

* * *

I will be using the following books as authoritative:

- For the New Testament, unless otherwise stated, *The Inclusive Bible: The First Egalitarian Translation* (Sheed and Ward, 2009).
- For the Hebrew Scriptures, unless otherwise stated,

The Holy Bible: New Revised Standard Version (Oxford University Press, 1989).

- For the translation of the Gospels of Philip, Thomas, and Mary Magdalene, with minimal alterations, Lynn C. Bauman, Ward J. Bauman, Cynthia Bourgeault, *The Luminous Gospels: Thomas, Mary Magdalene, and Philip* (Praxis Publishing, 2008).

PART ONE

THE *REORDERED* GOSPEL OF PHILIP

CHAPTER 1
THE JERUSALEM TEMPLE

1. Those who pray over Jerusalem, loving her because they already dwell within her, behold her as she now is. These are called the holiest of Holy Ones.

2. At the temple in Jerusalem there are three chambers to which one can bring an offering. One opens to the West called the Holy Place. The second opens to the South and is called the Holy of Holies, and the third opens to the East, which is the Holiest of all where only the High Priest may enter. Immersion or baptism brings one into the Holy Place. Restoration to fullness of being is the Holy of Holies, and the Holiest Place is the Bridal Chamber.

3. Immersion leads to resurrection, resurrection leads to the great restoration, and restoration leads to union in the Bridal Chamber, which transcends everything else, for nothing can be compared to it.

4. The veil in the Temple was torn in two to reveal the Bridal Chamber, which is nothing other than the image of the heavenly Temple. The curtain of the Temple on earth was torn from top to bottom, but it is entirely fitting for that which is below to move upward to that which is above.

5. At first the way in which God works to govern the

creation was covered by the Temple Veil, but once that veil was torn and what was inside revealed, the outer form of desolation was to be abandoned and left to be destroyed. Then everything was to flee those external places outside the Holy of Holies where it is impossible to unite with the Light or with the unflawed fullness. Instead, all were to come under the wings of the Cross and within the embrace of its arms. This is the ark of safety for us, a place of refuge when the waters of cataclysm overwhelm us.

6. In the priesthood there were those who were able to go inside behind the veil accompanied by the High Priest. So, for this reason, then, the veil was not torn simply at the top so that it would be available only to those who are higher. Nor was it torn at the bottom to bring revelation only to those who are lower. Rather, it was torn from top to bottom, opening to those both above and below that all might have access to the truth of hidden things.

7. This truth is important, and its excellence strengthens us to go inward through the symbols, humble and often rejected though they may be, and by this lowly means to enter into the presence of the fullness of glory—glory upon glory, light upon light, power upon power. Those who have reached this perfection open the way into the truth of hidden things for the rest of us, and thus saints and sacred beings bring us to the threshold of the Bridal Chamber and invite us within.

CHAPTER 2
THE HOLY PLACE

1. The names we give to things in this world create confusion and turn our hearts away from what is real to what is unreal. For example, the one who hears the name "God" does not perceive what is real but is made to think only of what is unreal. The same is true for the words Father, Son, Holy Spirit, life, light, resurrection, and church - all these terms take us away from reality into illusion. They succeed merely in leading humanity to death, for they exist only as constructs of this world. If, however, we were to exist in the *Aion*—that realm transcendent to space-time—then nothing named in this world would be considered evil, nor would we see ourselves merely as temporal creatures, for each being has a destiny in the Transcendent Realm (the *Aion*).

2. There is one name, however, that is unrepeatable in this world. It is the name "(Abba), Father" which has been given by means of a Son. This name is honored above all other names, and if this name had not been given to him as well, the Son could not become a "Father." Those who possess this name can perceive it, but never adequately speak of it, and those who do not possess it can never even conceive of it. For our sakes Truth begets names for everything in the world, and it is impossible to know anything without them.

3. One alone is truth and yet she makes the many, and by means of many things she lovingly teaches this one truth alone to all.

4. The Apostles before us called Yeshua the Nazarite, the Messiah, which means that Yeshua the Nazarite was the Anointed One. Of his names, the last is the title, the Anointed One (the Christ). The first is the name Yeshua, and the middle is Nazarite. The title Messiah has a double meaning. It is both the Anointed One, and one who has been weighed or measured out. Yeshua is a Hebrew word meaning salvation or restoration, and Nazar refers to the truth. The Nazarite, then, is the Truth who as the Anointed One measures out, and the Nazarite and Yeshua are the measurements.

5. The name "Yeshua" is the private name, and the "Christ" is the public or revealed name. Yeshua does not occur in other languages, but "the Christ" is "Messiah" in Aramaic, "Christos" in Greek, and its equivalent for "the Anointed One" in the languages of different peoples. He who has been revealed as the one consecrated to God, however, is the real secret, and as the Anointed One, he contains everything within his heart: the human, the archetype, the mystery, and the Father.

6. Some say that first the Master died and then was raised, but they are confused. First he was resurrected, and then he died. Those who are resurrected first are like God; they are already alive and can never die.

7. The names "Father" and "Son" are single words, and "Sacred Spirit" is, of course, double. The Father and the Son

exist everywhere, in transcendence above and in space-time below, in what is visible or manifest, and what is invisible and unmanifest. The Sacred Spirit, however, becomes visible when descending towards the material plane, and invisible when ascending towards transcendent realities.

8. Truth did not come to us in this world naked. Rather it was clothed with symbol and image, for it cannot be received in any other way. There is rebirth into another time, and there is the image of that rebirth, but it is truly imperative that one not be reborn in symbol only. So, what, then, is the resurrection and its image or symbol—for resurrection comes through the icon? And what is the image of the Bridal Chamber—for through its icon one is brought into the truth of the restoration of all things? It is crucial, then, not simply to come to birth through the Father, the Son and the Sacred Spirit in name only, but to be born through them in actuality. Whoever is not given birth by them will also have their names, which one received in the anointing that comes from the power of the cross, removed. These individuals have not simply received the anointing—which the Apostles called the union of opposites of the right and the left—but they have also themselves become "the Christ," the Anointed one.

9. The Master accomplished all this through the mysteries: Baptism, Anointing, Eucharist, restoration to fullness of being, and the Bridal Chamber, saying, "I have come to make the inner as the outer, and the outer as the inner." Everything he said he spoke by means of signs and images concerning that place which is transcendent to this one. And all those who confirm, "I am the Christ," also come from that transcendent place beyond confusion.

10. If one goes down into the water and comes up having received nothing and then says, “I too am the Christ,” he or she is Christian in name only and has simply taken the Name “on loan.” But if he or she receives the gift of the Sacred Spirit, then that Name has also been received as a gift, which can never be taken away, whereas a loan can always be recalled.

11. If you say, “I am a Jew,” no one will be surprised by that. If you say, “I am a Roman,” it will disturb no one. If you say, “I am a Greek, or a barbarian, a slave or a freeman,” no one will pay much attention. If, however, you say, “I am the Christ,” it will indeed cause a reaction. May it be that I receive whatever is needed to withstand in the cosmos when that is uttered.

12. The oil of anointing is superior to the waters of immersion, for because of the anointing we too are also called “the Christ” just as Yeshua was called the Anointed One because of the anointing oil. For the Father anoints the Son, and the Son anoints the Apostles, and the Apostles have anointed us. The One who was first anointed, however, received it completely: its resurrection, its light, its cross, and its Sacred Spirit. All of this the Father bestowed upon him in the Bridal Chamber, for he received it there. The Father lives in the Son and the Son lives in the Father. This, then, is the Realm of the Heavens.

13. A person of Jewish faith can make another person a Jew—called a convert, but a convert cannot make anyone else a Jew.

14. The truth is some beings can make other beings as receptive as themselves. While others have no such capacity, they simply are as they are.

15. God is a dyer in the same way that colors called true or permanent are used for dying the things placed into them. This is the heart of the matter—God uses dyes that are not perishable, but are permanent—immortal colors, and plunges those immersed in it into an abundance of water.

16. The Master went into the dye works of Levi and took seventy-two colors and threw them into a vat, but then what he drew up out of it was entirely white. "This," he said, "is the way in which the Son of Humanity comes to you as a dyer."

17. In a vision, one of the Apostles saw some who were shut up in a house on fire crying out with loud and fiery voices. They had been cast into the fire, but there was water there and they said to themselves, "is not the water here meant to save us from death?" Misled by their desires, death, which is called the "outer darkness," was their punishment.

18. Our enemy, therefore, comes to us from out of the waters with fire. And we ourselves have also come forth out of the water with soul and the Spirit and full of light, which is possessed by all the sons and daughters of the Bridal Chamber. Fire is also in the oil of anointing and light is within the fire. I am not speaking here, however, about light without form, but rather of the light whose appearance takes the form of a brilliant whiteness and is full of beauty, and whose glory gives beauty to everything else.

19. Likewise, the living water is itself a being in order that we might become clothed with that living body. It is for this reason, then, that whoever goes down into the water stripped naked, emerges out of it clothed with Divine Being.

20. It was in just this way that Yeshua perfected the water of baptism by emptying death out of it. For this reason we are made to go down into the water, not so that we might die, but in order that the spirit of this world might be poured away from us. For wherever the winds of the world blow it is always winter, but when the Sacred Spirit breathes it turns to summer.

21. From a place of profound understanding the Master said: "Some have attained the Realm of Heaven laughing." These came forth from out of this world rejoicing, for they went down into the water as anointed ones and rose out of it again as masters over all. They did not consider what they had done as some mere diversion. Instead, they cast off this world of impermanence in favor of the Heavenly Realm. Recognizing the world's order for what it is, a game being played, they rejected it, and emerged out of it laughing.

22. Those who go down into the waters of baptism are not immersed into death, but brought forth into the great restoration, which the Anointed One himself inaugurated by bringing those whom he called into its fulfillment through his Name. For it is in this way that he completes the right-relationship between all things.

23. Those who say that they will die and then be raised are confused. If while still alive they do not first enter the resurrection, they will receive nothing when they die. It is in this way, then, that we must understand the greatness of immersion, for those who receive it, live.

24. As long as evil is hidden and continues to contaminate the seed of the Sacred Spirit, it retains its full potency and is

capable of enslaving us by its oppressive force. But as soon as the Perfect Light shines forth pouring itself down upon us, those at its heart receive the anointing. It is precisely then that the slaves are freed and rescued from captivity.

25. There are those who are afraid of being resurrected stripped bare. Their desire, therefore, is to be raised in a material body, not realizing that someone clothed in flesh is actually naked. Those who have become beings of light, however, have put off the flesh and yet they are not bare.

26. However, I must oppose those who deny that neither form nor flesh shall rise from the dead, for both positions are in error—those who say the material form shall rise and those who say no form will ever rise. Here is what I affirm: those who say that it is the Spirit and the Light enfleshed which shall rise. This is because nothing can exist or even be said without taking form, and nothing can arise apart from it. Everything rises through some form of incarnation, for everything is held there in its very heart.

27. It has been said, "flesh and blood cannot inherit God's Kingdom." So what is it that cannot inherit that realm and what is it that can? What inherits the Kingdom is that which is in communion with Yeshua's blood—for it is he who said, "Whoever does not eat my flesh and drink my blood does not possess life." So what is this flesh? It is Logos. And what is this blood? It is the Sacred Spirit. Whoever receives these has both food and drink and is fully clothed.

28. Do not neglect the Lamb, for without him you will not be able to find the doorway, and no one can enter the presence of the King stripped bare.

29. In this world those who clothe themselves with outer garments are superior to the clothes they wear. In the heavenly realm, however, the clothing is superior to those who wear them for they have been clothed by water and purified entirely by fire.

30. Some things are exposed through revelation, and some are hidden in secret, while other things remain hidden even when revealed. Living water is hidden in baptismal water, and fire is hidden in the oil of anointing.

31. No one hides a thing of great value in something that will attract attention, but folk will often put objects of worth into a container that is worth little or nothing. Likewise, the soul—a precious thing—has come to exist in a humble body.

32. If a pearl is cast into the mud, it does not lose its value, nor does it have any greater value if it is rubbed with ointment. It is of immense worth to its owner no matter what befalls it at any time. So it is with the sons and daughters of God; regardless of what happens to them they are held as precious in the Father's heart.

CHAPTER 3
THE HOLY OF HOLIES

1. The Eucharistic chalice contains wine and water symbolizing the blood over which thanks is given. The cup, however, is filled with Spirit, which is for the perfecting of humanity. Whoever, therefore, drinks from the cup becomes a completed being.

2. Sacred beings are entirely holy, including their bodies. If such persons receive the Bread and Wine, they sanctify it, and everything else they touch is also purified. How is it possible then, that the body would not be pure as well?

3. Yeshua is the Eucharist Feast, because in Aramaic he is called *farisatha*—the One opened out and extended over all, for he came to bring the system of this world to death by means of the cross.

4. It is not possible for a person to see the higher realities of existence unless that person has become as real as they are. Not so, however, with individuals in this world. A person can see the sun without becoming the sun, or the heavens and earth without becoming them. Matters of truth, however, are different. What you see from beyond comes because you yourself are transcending toward them. You've seen the Spirit because you are becoming Spirit. You've seen the Anointed One because you yourself are becoming anointed. You've

seen the Father because you are becoming fatherly. However, in this world though you see everything, still you do not see yourself. Should you come to see yourself in that realm beyond this world, you would become what you see.

5. No one can see the reflection of themselves in water or in a mirror without light, and no one can see the light without water or a mirror to reflect it. To see one's true self, it is necessary to be immersed in both—the light as well as the water, and the light is present in the oil of anointing.

6. Is it not important that those in whom the fullness has come to dwell completely understand themselves? Those who do not know themselves, shall never enjoy what they possess. Those, however, who do come to understand who they are, will enjoy what they have.

7. When someone who is blind is in the dark with someone who can see they are no different from one another. But when the light comes, and that one who can see beholds the light, the blind person remains in the darkness still.

8. A donkey turning a millstone walks a hundred miles, but in the end it finds itself back at the same place it started. There are humans who likewise travel hither and yon, but who have made no progress anywhere. When darkness falls they cannot discern a city from a village, artifacts from nature, a lower power from a higher power. These wretched ones have labored in vain.

9. Yeshua took everyone by surprise, for he did not reveal himself as he truly was, but only according to the capacities of those who were able to perceive him. Though everyone

was susceptible to mortality, nevertheless, he revealed himself to all. To the great ones he revealed himself as great; to the little ones he became small. To angels he revealed himself as angel, to humanity as a man. Yet in all of these the Logos itself was the hidden secret, though some who saw him realized they were seeing themselves.

10. So when he revealed himself to his students in glory on the Mountain, he was no longer small, but great and enabled his students also to become great, so that they might perceive his nobility. On that day in an act of great thanksgiving he cried, "O You who have united Perfect Light with Sacred Spirit, come bind our angels to the icons."

11. When that which is from above comes into manifestation, it is commonly thought to be from below. When something is hidden or unmanifest, it is often said to be from above. It is important, therefore, that the interior and the exterior exist together beyond all externals, and for this reason the Master called the schism between them an "outer darkness" because transcendence cannot exist there. He also says, "My Father dwells in secret, so go into the hidden chamber and shut the door and commune there with the One who is in this hidden place within you." The Father is there in your innermost being and there is no other place transcendent to this, which is the Fullness beyond all "place."

12. Therefore, the Master said to his students, "Come, indeed, into the Abba's house, but do not take your possessions into it, and do not remove anything from it."

13. Before the Anointed One appeared, no one could return to that "place" from which they had come, and neither

could they leave this external place that they had entered. But when the Anointed One came, he brought interiority into the external world, and those caught within the outer world, he took inside.

14. In this world, one can exist either in the realm of resurrection, or in a domain between them. May it be that I am not found in the latter place! Both good and evil exist here, but the good is not an unmixed good, nor the evil pure evil. Yet in that region, which is death, pure evil does exist. So, while we are here in this world, it is to our advantage to be born into the resurrection, so that when the flesh is finally stripped away and we are naked, we shall find ourselves in the place of rest, and not wandering about in limbo. But on their earthly pilgrimage many do indeed go astray. Thus, it is good to come out of this world's system into that place where humankind existed before it became lost.

15. There are those, of course, who neither long for this, nor are they capable of accomplishing it. And still others who, though they wish for it, can never achieve it because they have no sustained practice. For it is "desire" itself, then, that turns many towards wrongdoing, and the absence of hunger for right-relatedness both blocks a deeper desire and the ability to bring it about.

16. Those who stray are both born of Spirit and yet led astray by Spirit, for it is through the Spirit as breath that the fire both blazes up and is extinguished.

17. Both vessels made out of glass as well as those made from clay come into being through fire. When glass vessels break, they can be remade because they are formed by

breath. When pottery breaks, however, it is destroyed, for it has been made without breath.

18. Realized human beings are invulnerable to captivity because they are invisible to the outer eye, for if they were visible, they could be taken by force. No one can be granted this grace, however, unless they are clothed in Perfect Light, saturating their being. Clad in Light, they can move forth into the cosmos as a Completed Being from out of the Bridal Chamber.

19. It is crucial, then, to become fully realized before moving beyond this world. Whoever receives this gift without achieving mastery in this domain will have no mastery in any other, moving forward through these transitions in an imperfect state. Only Yeshua knows what the destiny of such a person will be.

20. Abraham rejoiced to see what he saw, and as a sign, he cut off the flesh of his foreskin to show us what it means to put away the fleshly system of this world.

21. In this world when any living entity holds their inner reality in secret, they live; when it is exposed, they die. For example, when the inner parts of a human are enclosed within the body, the person lives, but if they should become exposed to the external world, the person dies. So it is with a tree. If it sprouts in a normal manner, it will bud out and thrive as long as its roots are covered, but if it is uprooted and they are exposed, the tree withers and dies. This is true for everything brought into existence in this world, whether external and manifest, or internal and unmanifest.

22. If, for example, the roots of evil are hidden they remain strong, but as soon as they are recognized openly for what they are, they perish. It is because of this that the Logos says, "The axe has already been applied to the root of the tree." It will not merely fell the tree, however, for a tree chopped down will sprout from its roots again. Rather the axe bites down deep into the roots until they are exposed, and so Yeshua uproots them from their place, which has only been done in part by others.

23. Let us delve deeply into our own hearts to the root of evil and tear it out. If it is recognized for what it is, it will be uprooted. Yet if we are unconscious of it and do not recognize it, indeed it takes root within the heart and produces its own fruits there. It masters us and we are made its slaves. It captures us causing us to do things we would not do otherwise—and keeps us from doing what we truly desire. Its potency remains as long as we do not recognize it. Hidden and unconscious it coerces us.

24. Saints and sages are often served even by oppressive powers which have been blinded by the Sacred Spirit. These powers imagine that it is they who are affecting humanity when in fact they are actually serving sacred beings. It is for this reason that once when one of his students asked the Master concerning an issue involving this world, he replied, "Ask your Mother. She will give you something coming from other worlds."

25. The Apostles said this to their students, "May our offerings be salted." They called "salt," wisdom, for without its savor nothing is acceptable. Yet wisdom itself remains barren

without a son. She is called "Mother," therefore, because in her there is salt which has been found for us by the Sacred Spirit who assists in making many children.

26. That which the Father possesses belongs also to the children, but as long as they remain in their infancy, nothing is ever entrusted to them. When, however, they mature, all that the Father possesses he willingly gives to them.

27. The wisdom which some call barren, is herself the Mother of Angels.

28. Wisdom is one reality and death is another. (Wisdom, *khomath*, in Aramaic is simply *Sophia* in Greek). From death comes the wisdom of death, so that those acquainted with death do indeed possess a certain kind of wisdom, though it is a minor one.

29. Those who gain wisdom from truth are liberated beings, and a liberated being is one who does not habitually transgress—transgressors being slaves of their own offenses. Truth is our Mother and knowledge of her comes through joining with her. Those to whom Truth is given no longer offend, so the world calls them "free!" They cease their transgressions because they have gained wisdom from Truth, which raises the level of their hearts, and having transcended their state in the world, they are free indeed. Love, however, is what uplifts and frees them, and yet in their freedom true knowledge also makes them slaves of love on behalf of those who are not yet ready to live in the freedom of truth. Still, it is this knowledge which prepares them so that they too may become free beings.

30. Love possesses nothing, for how could it when everything already belongs to it? It never says, "This is mine," or "That belongs to me." It says instead, "All of this is yours."

31. Spiritual love is truly a fragrance-filled wine meant to be enjoyed by all who receive it, and those anointed with it share it with anyone who stands together with them. As long as they stand together, all are anointed by its healing ointment. Should they cease to stand together, however, then those not yet anointed will find themselves still deep in their own stagnation. Did not the good Samaritan give the wounded man wine mixed with oil, and with that anointing was he not healed from his wounds? For "love shall cover a multitude of sins."

32. Faith receives and love gives. Without faith no one can receive, and no one can give who does not love. We are, therefore, made to trust in order that we may receive, and caused to love in order that we might give. For if one gives without love, there is no benefit in the giving.

33. Anyone unreceptive to the transcendent continues on in lower realities.

CHAPTER 4
THE BRIDAL CHAMBER

1. Ignorance grounded in confusion is the mother of evil. Anyone working out of ignorance is not, was not, nor will ever be a true being. And yet, if truth is fully revealed, even these can be brought to perfection. Truth, like ignorance, if it is held in secret remains at rest within itself, but if it is manifest outwardly, then it becomes known and is superior because it triumphs over ignorance and liberates us from confusion. The Logos said, "You shall know the truth and the truth will set you free." It is ignorance that enslaves us, and enlightenment, which liberates us. When we come to recognize the truth, we will discover its fruits within our hearts. If we unite intimately with it, we shall reach ultimate fulfillment.

2. At present we are surrounded by the visible manifestations of creation. Some call these strong and valuable, while what is unseen or unknown is deemed weak and contemptible. The truth is, however, that what is manifest is weak and inferior, while what is unseen is powerful and praiseworthy.

3. Yet it is from the unseen world that the mysteries of truth are revealed through iconic images, but the Bridal Chamber itself remains hidden for it is the Holy of Holies.

4. This is the way one lives into the mysteries. There is magnificence to the mystery of marital union, for the world

is a complex system based upon humankind, and human society itself is grounded in marriage. So, contemplate, then, instead the union of pure spiritual embrace, for it has great power. Its image, however, is found in physical sexual union.

5. Let not the Bridal Chamber be for animals, slaves, or harlots. Rather, let it be for those both free and virginal!

6. Indeed, we have been begotten and brought into being by the aid of the Sacred Spirit, and then we were reborn by means of the Anointed One. In both cases it is Spirit who has anointed us, and having thus been reborn, we are now "married" beings.

7. There are those who say that Mary conceived by means of the Sacred Spirit. They are confused and know not of what they speak. When has it ever occurred that the female has conceived by means of the feminine? Mary, who was honored among the Jewish and other Apostles, was not impregnated by a feminine power. Any power seeking to do that only defiles itself. So, the Master would not have said, "My father in heaven," unless he had an earthly father. He would simply have called him, "Abba."

8. There were three named "Miriam" who continuously walked with the Master: his mother, his sister, and Magdalene who was called his companion. Thus, Miriam is his mother, his sister, and his mate.

9. The companion of the Anointed One was Miriam of Magdala, for the Master appeared to love her more than the other students, and many times would kiss her on the

mouth. When the others saw his love for her they asked him, "Why do you love her more than the rest of us?" "Do not I love you as I love her?" the Savior answered.

10. All those born in this world are begotten physically, but there are those who are also born of Spirit. Those begotten in God's heart are called and nourished there in order that they might reach the promised destiny of transcendence. Grace flows from his mouth—the source of the Logos, which also nourishes us in order that we might become complete. Fully realized human beings are, thus, conceived through a kiss, and then they are born. We should desire, therefore, to kiss one another and assist in each other's conception through the love we mutually share.

11. Horses naturally give birth to horses, humans to humans, and God gives birth to God. This is the way that sons and daughters are born from the Lover and Beloved in the Bridal Chamber. Jews did not come into being from Greeks, and Christians came into being not from Jews, but from other anointed ones. It is good, then, to call the offspring who have been chosen by the Sacred Spirit, the "True Humanity" and "Sons and Daughters of the Human One," born from the seed of the Son of Humanity. This new race bears the name "True human" in this world, and it is here, in this very place, where they become the sons and daughters of the Bridal Chamber.

12. The child who is born of a woman resembles the one she loves. If it is her husband, then it resembles him, but if she has an extra-marital lover, well, then it looks like him. Strangely, if a woman lies with her husband because he has coerced her yet her heart is elsewhere, her offspring

will resemble the other one she loves. Those who go in to be with the Son of God are not in love with the system of this world, but rather with the Master, and so those who are conceived by him resemble him, and not this world.

13. It is natural for humans to unite with humans, horses with horses, and donkeys with donkeys. Species unite with like species in the same manner that Spirit unites with Spirit, Logos with Logos, and Light with Light. If you become human, you will be loved by humans. If you become Spirit, the Spirit will unite with you. If you become Logos, the Logos will come to you. If you become Light, the Light will become a companion to you. If you transcend, then Transcendence itself will rest upon you. If, however, you become horse-like, or behave like a donkey, calf, dog, sheep, or any other creature outside of or lower than yourself, you will be incapable of being loved by what is either human, Spirit, Logos, or Light, by what is transcendent to you, or by what is deeply immanent within you. None of these will be able to find rest within your heart, nor will you find a place of residence within theirs.

14. The powers that be can do nothing against those who have been clothed in Perfect Light. They can neither see nor seize them, for they have been vested with light through the mysteries of spiritual marriage.

15. Anyone who is born a child from the Bridal Chamber shall receive the Light, for if one does not receive it there, there is nowhere else to receive it. Those who welcome the Light are hidden from the world, and cannot, therefore, be controlled or troubled by it. Such beings have already received the Truth through the image of the icons and

whether they leave this world or act within it in a public way, it has already become for them the Great Age of the Eternal Now whose fullness is no longer hidden by the darkness of night, but has burst forth revealing itself to them, to be hidden now, as holy Light within Perfect Day.

16. In the days when the feminine Eve was held within the masculine Adam, there was no death, but when they were separated out from one another, then death came into existence. But if, once again, she returns inward and he receives her inside, death shall cease to be.

17. If the female had not been separated from the male, she would never have died with the male. Her separation, however, became the cause and origin of death. It is for this reason that the Anointed One came that he might remedy this condition by uniting the masculine and the feminine together again. When the feminine and the masculine come together in spiritual union within the Bridal Chamber, therefore, they are no longer separated—a separation which occurred when Adam and Eve united outside the Bridal Chamber.

18. Adam's soul was brought into being by the Breath whose spouse is the Anointed One. The Spirit gave Adam his soul, for she is the soul's mother. But because he had not yet been united to the Logos, the dominant powers were able to deceive him. Still, all those who unite to the Sacred Spirit in the secret place within are invited one by one into the Bridal Chamber where they are joined in spiritual marriage.

19. There are both male and female spirits, which at heart are unclean or impure. Male spirits seek to mate with souls that

inhabit a female form, and female spirits seek an unequal relationship with a male form. So, no one, then, is able to escape being seized by their compulsions if they have not received both the power of the male and the female in equal balance. It is in the iconic Bridal Chamber, where the bride is united with the bridegroom that this balance is attained. Outside that union, unwisely females see a lone male and begin to flirt with him until they are engaged in sexual relations. Likewise, males who see a beautiful female by herself will, out of lust, try to seduce and then sexually coerce her. Yet when the male and female sit side-by-side together in mutuality, neither will coerce the other nor be coerced. This only occurs when the image and the Archetype are united in mutuality.

20. There are, of course, those who pray frequently, "O keep us safe from the unclean and demonic forces, for we are the faithful ones!" But if they had only possessed the Sacred Spirit, nothing unclean would ever cling to them. So, neither fear the flesh nor love it. For if you fear it, it will become your master, and if you love it, it will devour and suffocate you.

21. And so in this world, even where the forces are strong, they are not able to seize hold of one who has manifestly transcended both the fear and the force of the flesh. This individual's self-mastery is so precious an element that they are able to withstand the violent reactions of the multitudes that wish to seize and suffocate them out of envy. Are not such individuals able then to escape through the divine reality? Are they, then, ever really afraid?

22. When the Master cried from the cross, "My God, My God, why have You abandoned me," he was separated below

from that which was above—from what had originally been begotten together and brought forth by God through the Sacred Spirit.

23. But when the Master rose from death and was as he had been before, except now he came in a body that had been perfected, He was still incarnated in flesh, but this time in a new kind of flesh, which in our present incarnation we have not yet reached, remaining only images of what is real.

24. The Son of Humanity exists, as do the children of the Son. The Son of Humanity is the Master who has brought the children into created being. The Son of Humanity, therefore, has received the power to both create and beget. That which he creates is, of course, a finite object—a creature, but what he begets, however, is a "child"—or offspring. Created objects are not able to conceive, but what has been conceived and born can create. Some will say, "Well, human creatures, of course, do conceive and give birth." True, but their progeny are in fact creatures, and what they give birth to are not "theirs," but sons and daughters of God.

25. The one who creates objects works outwardly in the external world. The one who labors in secret, however, works within the icon, hidden inwardly from others. The one who creates makes objects visible to the world. The one who conceives gives birth to children in the Realm of the Unseen.

26. Adam was formed in creation and then there were those begotten through him, but you cannot find nobility in his progeny. If Adam had been begotten instead of made, his seed would likewise have been noble-minded, but he was

made, and they were begotten so where is the nobility? First there occurred adultery and then murder, for the slayer was begotten in adultery, being the son of the serpent. Thus, he became a murderer like his true father and killed his brother. Any partnership, therefore, between unlike beings is a form of adultery.

27. Transcendent Humanity has far more sons and daughters than earthly humanity. If the sons and daughters of Adam are a multitude even though they continually die, how many more are the offspring of the Completed Human who do not die but are continually being born?

28. The Father is the source of the Son, but it is impossible for the Son to be the origin of the other sons. The one who is begotten, then, is not the source of other children: rather he assists in bringing his own siblings into being.

29. The truth regarding the deeds of humanity is this: Deeds come from human power called "abilities," but another "accomplishment" of humans is the progeny born to them from out of a period of rest. Through power humans are able to govern, and yet children also reveal accomplishment, though they come from this state of repose. You will see, then, that this applies all across the imagery used to mirror human beings: personal accomplishment is done through effort or power, and yet through rest or repose children are begotten.

30. In this world slaves are forced to work for those who are free-born. In the Realm of the Heavens, however, it is the free-born who act to serve the slaves—for children born from the Bridal Chamber bear the same name—Rest. And

they share it mutually and need nothing else, for in their awareness they contemplate the glorious beauty of the icons. This is true immortality, for these dwell in the sacred Bridal Chamber receiving all the glory of those who have reached fulfillment.

31. No one but the couple themselves knows when they will come together in intimate union. Marriage therefore is a mystery for anyone in this world who has taken a mate. If natural union occurs in secret, how much greater is the hidden mystery of spiritual marriage which takes place in truth rather than in flesh, out of pure love rather than in passionate lust, in the full light of day rather than in the darkness of night. When sexual union is put on public display it becomes pornographic. When a woman who has conjugal relations with another man or seeks for such outside her home is found out, she is known as a prostitute.

32. A woman may only reveal herself to her mother and father, to the "friend" of the bridegroom, or to the "children" of the bridegroom, for only these may enter daily into the Bridal Chamber. As to all the rest, let them long simply to hear her voice, catch a brief scent of her fragrance, or like dogs find crumbs that fall from her table. It is only the Lover and the Beloved that belong in the Bridal Chamber. No one else can behold them there unless they too become Bride and Groom.

33. So then every seed that my Father in heaven has not planted shall be uprooted. Those who were separated shall be united, and all who are empty shall be filled, so that everyone may enter into the Bridal Chamber where they will be born into the Light. Their birth shall not be as a result of

some unseen union that flares up like a fire in the night and then is extinguished, but rather as the result of the mystery of Spiritual Marriage, is consummated in the full light of day, whose light never ceases nor shall ever be put out.

CHAPTER 5
THE COSMOS

1. At the river Jordan Yeshua revealed the great fullness that is the Kingdom of the Heavens, which existed before all things. There he was begotten as the Son. There he was anointed. There he was restored to fullness of being. And from there he began the great restoration.

2. So, let us speak then of this great mystery in this way: The Father of All came down and united with the virgin, and on that day made light shine forth from the fire—revealing to us the power of the Bridal Chamber. Because of this, also on that day Yeshua came into fullness of being, coming forth from the Bridal Chamber as a bridegroom with his bride. It was also in this way that the balance of All was established in Yeshua's heart so that by means of this each of his students might have access to enter into his Rest.

3. How then does Yeshua give rest to everyone? First of all, he brings sorrow and grief to no one whether great or small, or whether it be a believer or an unbeliever. Rather he gives rest to those who reside among the Good. Some indeed are privileged to bring rest to those who are virtuous, but there are those who do well and yet cannot of themselves give repose to anyone since their goodness was not accomplished by an act of will. There are those who are in pain, but again he is not oppressing them. There are times when

grief does come to the virtuous, not because he oppresses them, but because their own flaws and calamities have overwhelmed them. It is natural, then, to give joy to those who are good, yet some must endure terrible grief.

4. The Anointed One has come! And in coming some he ransoms, others he releases and restores, and there are those whom he rescues. He ransomed strangers and made them his own. Those who came to him he restored. All this he gave as a self-offering out of his own love and desire. Not only did he willingly give himself at his appearing, from the very beginning of the cosmos it was his longing to do so. And so now in this way he comes to receive back what he has always loved—releasing all who were held captive by thieves of the soul, redeeming everything in the cosmos, both good and evil.

5. It is grace, then, which has caused the humble of the earth to reign over heaven. These have been received into the Realm of the Blessed where the Logos has uplifted their souls. For it is Yeshua, the Anointed One, who has seduced and beguiled us all, and yet he has never coerced or oppressed anyone, and because of this the Blessed Ones become fully realized human beings as well as the Logos. If you should ask us about such beings, any attempt to correctly portray their grandeur would be difficult.

6. Light exists with darkness, life with death. The right hand and the left hand belong together as siblings. It is not possible, then, to separate them from their mutual complementarity. Good is never entirely good, nor evil pure evil, or life without death, nor death without life. Each entity unfolds towards its origin from the beginning point, and

everything which transcends this world is no longer mortal, but is brought forth into eternal reality.

7. The embrace of opposites occurs in this world: masculine and feminine, strength and weakness. In the Great Age—the *Aion*—something similar to what we call embrace occurs as well, but though we use the same name for it, forms of union there transcend what can be described here. For in that place there exists that which is stronger than the greatest force and those who are superior to all force.

8. There is being and there is non-being, but Reality is One and Whole, but still it is not able to enter into anyone who only has a heart of flesh.

9. This world devours its dead and those who are eaten die from within, at the level of the heart. Truth, however, is fed by life and so anyone who is nourished by it will never die. Yeshua has come to us from that Realm of Truth and has brought us true food, and to those desiring it he gave them back their lives again so that they may never die.

10. Before the coming of the Anointed One, no bread from paradise—that place where Adam had first been created—existed in this world. There was all manner of plants for the nourishment of the wild creatures, but there was no wheat for humanity who had only the food provided for all the rest. But when the Anointed came as the Completed Human, he brought bread from heaven so that humanity could be nourished with its own true food. The authorities imagined, of course, that it was through their own force of will they had provided it. Yet all along in secret it was the Sacred Spirit who had been energizing everything in whatever manner

she desired. So then truth from its very beginning has been scattered everywhere. Many have watched it being sown, but few who have seen it have reaped it.

11. The world's system as we know it fell away from those who made it. Their ambition was that it be imperishable and deathless. Those who created it, however, never realized their ambitions, for they themselves fell away. There is, therefore, nothing deathless or immortal about the system of this world, nor about those who created it.

12. Things certainly exist, but they are impermanent. Only true sons and daughters, then, can attain immortality, and no one can gain eternity without first becoming a true son or daughter. Those who have received this gift, how can they possibly give it away?

13. The overarching powers wish to deceive humanity knowing that we have a natural kinship to that which is truly good. They take the very word "good" and apply it to things that are not good, so that words themselves deceive and enslave us. Yet, when grace comes and we are removed from all that is tainted and placed back with the Good, we recognize ourselves for who we truly are. Being free, the powers seek to take and make us slaves to themselves through time. Because the Authorities seek to control and enslave us so that we will not recognize our true reality, divine power has been granted humanity.

14. Wherever humanity exists, slavery exists, so in the past, when sacrifices began, animals were offered up to divine power. These were living things offered up alive, only to be

killed. One human, however, was offered up to God dead, and yet now he lives.

15. A slave longs only for freedom and not for his Master's fortune, but a son is not only a child of the Master, he is an heir with claim to his father's wealth. Likewise, children of death are not only dead, death is their only inheritance. Heirs of life, on the other hand, are themselves alive, and they can inherit both life and death. The dead, however, inherit nothing, for how can a dead person become an heir? But if those who are dead should inherit life, not only will they live, they will never die.

16. A citizen of this world, in fact, cannot die for he or she has actually never lived, but one who has begun to know the truth is fully alive—having come to life on the day of the Anointed One's appearing; that individual, however, may well face the danger of dying, for this world's system is a construct, adorning itself with cities, from which they carry out the dead. In our early Jewish days we remained orphaned, having only a mother, but when we became followers of the Anointed One, for our sakes the Father joined our Mother.

17. Those who have been enslaved against their will, are able to be liberated while those who by the grace of their Master have been freed and yet sell themselves back into slavery, shall forfeit their freedom.

18. God created the garden of paradise and humankind dwelt there, but God's desires were not in their hearts. Their longings were elsewhere. And in this garden, it was

said—even to me—"You may eat of this, but you cannot consume that, though you desire it." That is the place, therefore, where I myself ate many different things, and also the place where the Tree of Knowledge killed Adam. Yet it is that same Tree of Knowledge which shall also enliven humanity.

19. In the past, the commandments were the Tree for they gave us knowledge of what is good and evil, but they could not cure humanity of evil, nor preserve us in that which is good. Instead, they caused those who took them into their hearts to die. And so, the commandment, "Eat this! Do not eat that!" became the origin of death.

20. It is said by the Apostle Philip that Joseph the Carpenter planted a grove of trees in his garden because he needed the wood for his craft. And from the trees he had planted the cross was made, and on that cross his own seed hung. The seed was Yeshua, and what he planted became the cross. Yet the Tree of Life exists in the midst of the garden of paradise, and it also is an olive tree from whose heart the oil of anointing flows into the resurrection.

21. Adam came into being from two virgins: the Spirit and the virgin Earth. The Anointed One, therefore, was also born of a virgin so that the stumbling, which occurred at the beginning, might be rectified.

22. There are two trees in paradise: the one produces beasts, and the other produces humankind. It was Adam who ate from the tree producing beasts and so he himself not only became bestial but gave birth to the same. Because of this, human beings began to worship animals. It was in this way,

also, that Adam took from the fruit of that tree and multiplied and distributed it, so by eating its fruit, humans gave birth to humans, and also began to worship other humans.

23. It was God, however, who created human beings, but it was humans who created their own gods. So this has been the way it is in this world; humans create their own gods and worship them. It would be far more fitting if the gods of their own creation worshiped humans instead!

24. People have been sacrificed to gods who "devoured" human beings. Before humans, animals were sacrificed to these so-called "divinities." Whoever receives such sacrifices, however, is not in fact divine.

25. Consider a landowner of means who has children, servants, cattle, hogs, and dogs, as well as wheat, barley, hay, fodder, meats, and acorns. Being wise he understands the nutritional needs of each member of his household. To children he gives bread, olive oil and meat. To servants he offers oil and grain. To cattle he gives barley, hay, and fodder. He throws bones to the dogs and acorns and bread crusts to the pigs. So, it is with spiritual masters. If they are wise and truly understand the principle of discipleship they will not be fooled by outer physical form or appearance; rather they will perceive the inner condition of each individual's soul and will adjust their words accordingly.

26. In our world's system there are many humans who take on animal characteristics. The wise recognize this and to swine-like beings they throw acorns. To those who are bovine in nature, they give barley, straw, and hay. To those

whose characteristics are canine, bones. To servants, however, they give basic fare, and to their offspring they offer complete food.

27. Among animals there are those such as oxen and donkeys as well as others, which are submissive to human beings, and there are those in the wild which are not. We feed ourselves and provide for both tame and wild animals by plowing the fields with those submissive to us. In the same way the first Realized Human Being makes use of the powers submissive to him to bring everything in existence under cultivation, and for this reason whatever there is whether for good or ill, on the right hand or on the left, exists. It is, however, the Sacred Spirit who shepherds each separate being and who commands both the submissive as well as the wild and lonely powers so that she is able to control and use their energies even beyond their own desires.

28. The Master said, “Blessed are all who existed before coming into being, for all who are now both existed before and shall ever be.”

29. The transcendence of human beings is not obvious to the naked eye. It remains hidden from view, but the result is that humans have mastery over creation, even over those creatures which are larger and stronger. Through what is visible and what is hidden, we are able to survive.

30. When, however, humans separate from nature, then everything begins to devour and destroy itself because there is no mutual nourishment. But when human beings cherish and cultivate the earth, then all things are properly fed.

31. Those who sow in winter reap in summer. Winter symbolizes the world-system, and summer, the Great Age, the realm of transcendence. Let us sow, therefore, in this world that we may reap in the summertime. For this reason, we are not asked to pray for harvest in the wintertime, but for the summer, which comes from winter. If one tries to reap in the wintertime, it only uproots the field and there is no harvest. This approach is fruitless since nothing emerges in the winter, and as a result, in that other realm—the true Sabbath—the fields become barren.

32. In this world crops are cultivated and gathered into barns using four elements: soil, water, wind, and light. Likewise, God also cultivates the world through the elements of trust, hope, love, and enlightenment. Our soil is the heart where trust takes root. Hope is the water through which we are nourished. Love is the wind by which we grow, and enlightenment is the Light which causes us to ripen.

PART TWO

THE PHILIP MYSTERIES EXPLORED

BEFORE WE BEGIN

According to the eighteenth chapter of the Gospel of John, during his trial Jesus said to Pilate, "I was born and came into the world for one purpose—to bear witness to the truth. Everyone who seeks the truth hears my voice." Pilate then asked Jesus, "Truth? What is truth?"

This is the primary question for all seekers and the germinal concern of the Gospel of Philip, as well. What is truth? How do we know what we know? Where is truth to be found and how can human consciousness perceive it? Philip says:

> One alone is truth, and yet she makes the many, and by means of many things she lovingly teaches this one truth alone to all (2:3).

In other words, the more we know of many things, the more we know of God. Truth is found in the great multiplicity of creation itself, guiding us to its fundamental principle that "Reality is One and Whole" (5:7). Philip's good news is that this essential knowledge is God's gift to humanity—and the direct path to our self-understanding.

We hear evidence of the Jewish roots of this second-century community of Christians: "Hear, O Israel, Adonai is our God, Adonai is One." (Deuteronomy 6:4)[1] Oneness is the essential reality we will come to understand as we learn

[1] Mishkan T'Filah: *A Reform Siddur* (Central Conference of American Rabbis, 2007), 34.

from Philip. God is One, though experienced in multitudinous ways. Philip's primary teaching is that all is One, and the One is in all. And in the many manifestations we call nature, we find our pedagogy, teaching us always and consistently the truth of the unity of all created things.

Outer forms of creation are not real in themselves, but rather icons of reality, pointing always to the intrinsic truth buried within everything and everyone. These external materializations fade and die, but what is veritable is unfazed by time and space. Physical separation and distinctions are illusions. The truth and reality of everything is its vital spiritual nature. When we each discover our own essential being we will know that God is One and, we'll come to see, so are we—one in the One, for there is no other.

CHAPTER 1
JERUSALEM TEMPLE, MYSTICAL TEMPLE, AND TEMPLE VEIL

The Gospel of Philip is a mysterious text and even beyond its disorder in our Coptic version there's much inexplicableness in deciphering its deepest meanings. Buried under centuries of historical detritus and cultural mutations it is beyond the scope of an amateur sleuth to dig through the mountains of striations to reach a true understanding of what was written and meant. It is only through prayerful engagement and scrupulous application that something of value can emerge.

JERUSALEM TEMPLE

As explained in the General Introduction, I believe this text to be a Jewish/Christian mystical primer whose purpose is to initiate neophytes into the Christian mysteries. The focal point is the metaphysical knowledge of the Jerusalem Temple, "the House of God." I believe Philip is organized around this perspective and should be read through this lens; thus, this passage on the Jerusalem Temple is the prologue to this Gospel and thus the first chapter of my reordering of the text.

The opening verse of this Gospel reveals the lens through which we will understand what is otherwise inscrutable: **"Those who pray over Jerusalem, loving her because they**

***already* dwell within her, behold her as she is *now*"** (1:1, italics mine). The focal point is this present moment, where we are right now. It immediately lifts our vision from the historical and lost Temple in Jerusalem to a present living reality where we potentially "already dwell." It raises our sights above the historic physical realm, where we most often live, to the transcendent possibility of our humanity. Those who have experienced this indwelling—for transcendence is an enlargement of human perception—have reaped the result of this iconic work. The Temple now having become an icon of our anthropic condition. Jesus initiated this mystical knowledge when he famously said to the Temple authorities, as found in the Gospel of John (2:19,21): "'Destroy this temple, and in three days I will raise it up.' But the temple he was speaking of was his body."

The iconic work here is prayer, that is, communion with the divine presence within the temple of our own being. This is the new Jerusalem, and only participants can comprehend this amazing insight. Central to this knowledge is the reality that we carry within us the *Shekinah*, the presence of the Holy One, and can thus bring that presence actively into our immediate physical environment. Those who find this transcendence, participating in God, fulfill God's reign upon the earth, and are, thus "the holiest of Holy Ones."

The tenth-century Byzantine monk, Symeon the New Theologian, speaks of this experience: "How do I adore You within myself and yet I perceive You at a distance? How do I embrace You within me and I see You in the heavens? You alone know it, You, the author of these things who shine like the sun in my heart, my material heart, immaterially. You who made the light of Your glory shine on me, O my God, through Your apostle, your disciple, your servant, the great saint Symeon. You Yourself shine still today in me and teach me to compose to God hymns at once both new and old, divine and secret, so that, through me, Your knowledge will be proclaimed marvelous, O my God, and that Your wisdom, Your great wisdom, shall shine still more, and then all will praise You, O my Christ, on hearing, that I speak in new languages by Your grace."[1]

The Jerusalem Temple, based on sacred architecture, was three-chambered. The first chamber, the court, called by Philip "the Holy Place," was open to the public. It was where all could come to pray and where sacrifices were made. The second chamber Philip calls "the Holy of Holies." It held the table of burnt offerings and was a sanctum for assembly. The innermost chamber, which Philip says is "the Holiest of Holy Places," was where the ancient, sacred ark of the covenant was kept, thus the Shekinah (Presence of God) was believed to reside there, and only the high priest could enter on the Day of Atonement for the expiation of sins. A linen veil separated the second chamber from the holiest place.

But in 70 CE, Roman soldiers destroyed the Temple, leveling the buildings and plundering its contents, thus destroying the center of Jewish worship and practice.

MYSTICAL TEMPLE

The names Philip gives to these three chambers are given to show anyone familiar with the scriptural accounts that Philip is speaking metaphorically, not historically. The temple Philip is revealing is the sacred temple of a human being, our own bodies.

---

[1] George A. Maloney, *Saint Symeon the New Theologian: The Mystic of Fire and Light and Hymns of Divine Love,* (IJA Publications, 2011), Hymn 7, 192.

For this Jewish sect of Philip-Christians, the Jerusalem Temple took on symbolic meaning, as it did for many non-Christian Jews. In the Gospel of Philip, the temple is a template of the heavenly temple, and the prototype of humanity. Not only does it reveal the truth of human anthropology but the mystery of the universe, and how the cosmos is restored to wholeness. A prayer of the eighth-century Syrian desert hermit, Isaac the Syrian, reflects this:

> O God, the heaven and the highest heavens do not contain you, yet you chose from us a rational Temple for your dwelling place; hold me worthy to become a dwelling place for your love—a love at the perception of which saints have forgotten themselves in their love for You.[2]

The secret that is revealed in this divine blueprint, is that humans are microcosms of the macrocosm, the "Kingdom of the Heavens." Roughly tripartite, as was the Jerusalem Temple, for Philip this reveals stages in human consciousness: the mind, the soul, and the most sacred and secret place—the heart—also called the "Bridal Chamber" by Philip. The fourteenth-century German mystic Meister Eckhart, in one of his German sermons, speaks of this innermost chamber in answer to a theoretical question:

> "Sir, Where is the silence [you are speaking of] and where is the place where the word is spoken?": It is in the purest thing that the soul is capable of, in the noblest part, the ground—indeed, in the very essence of the soul which is

[2] Sabastian Brock, *Headings on Spiritual Knowledge: Isaac of Nineveh* (St. Vladimir's Seminary Press, 2022), 92.

> the soul's most secret part. There is the silent "middle."[3]

Rather than representing physical chambers within a human person, these chambers are instead degrees of enlightenment, each bringing increasing depths of knowledge. As I gain new wisdom and understanding, guided by the Holy Spirit, my conscious level broadens, preparing me for ever greater knowledge. Ultimately, I am brought into spiritual awareness to such an extent that I am prepared for the true knowledge of God—which is the goal of this initiation.

The Christian mysteries, which Philip names as Baptism, Anointing, Eucharist, and Marriage, are iconic therefore, and pedagogical. That is, they are images of what is real and are given to reveal the profound inner experience to us.

As in all images, we should not see these images as ends in themselves. They do not yield their truths until we have actively participated in the invitation they offer. Each is a door revealing a further step into our transcendent state, that is, knowledge of God. But we will not and cannot become what they are promising until we have entered and partaken of their innate knowledge.

The outer physical experience prepares our souls for the inner work. The goal is that we give birth to the Christ, participating in the grand scheme of things. From the beginning of creation, the Creator has been birthing the Word (*Logos*), the Christ, and our participation today is essential. For, as Meister Eckhart put it long ago, what good is it for me if Christ was born through Mary in Bethlehem, "unless

[3] M. O'C. Walshe, *Meister Eckhart Sermons and Treatises, Volumes 1-3* (Element Books, 1987). Vol. 1, Sermon 1, 3.

I bear him too" into my world today?[4] "It is not possible for a person to see the higher realities of existence unless that person has become as real as they are" (Philip 3:4).

The first stage

The first stage (or chamber) of consciousness—accessed through the portal of Baptism and Anointing—Philip calls **resurrection**. Resurrection is a spiritual awakening, represented by a new commitment to a deeper spiritual endeavor. This is the beginning of a journey bringing me into a new state of being, based on new knowledge about myself. Ultimately, all creation is to be "resurrected," according to Philip. That is, made conscious of its intrinsic divine spiritual nature.

The second stage

The second stage of consciousness—accessed through the portal of the Eucharist—Philip calls **restoration to fullness of being**. This is a new, prayerful engagement with the Spirit of God within me, transforming my understanding and reforming my life.

The third stage

The third stage—accessed through the portal of Marriage—is a state of being found in the ground of my own soul, called **sacred marriage**, where communion with God has brought me into greater conformity with God and my own essential being. This is the highest form of the human mystical experience for it gives me a true knowledge of God and simultaneously I discover my true self as I become a fully realized human being. This marriage results in a new birthing of the

---

[4] Walshe, *Meister Eckhart Sermons and Treatises, Volume 2*, Sermon 88, 282.

Christ into my world. Having now found my sovereignty, I have become the Christ. God and I are one.

Again, Meister Eckhart echoes these ancient ideas:

> Wherein lies this true possession of God—this *really* having God? This true possession of God depends on the mind, an inner mental turning and striving toward God—but not in a continuous and equal thinking of God, for that would be impossible for nature to strive for, very difficult and not even the best thing. A person should not have, or be satisfied with, an imagined God, for then, when the idea vanishes God vanishes? Rather, one should have an essential God, who far transcends human thoughts. [An essential God] never vanishes unless a person willfully turns away from God.[5]

According to Philip, humans have evolved consciously and are thus ready and able to follow Jesus into a full realization of the human experience. Philip teaches us that much of our growth and development has been unconscious, but this spiritual work of transcendence requires our assent to follow Christ, who is our mentor, teacher, and guide. Early humans could not know the secrets of the soul and God's presence within. They were not ready. There was a veil over their consciousness. But that veil has been removed by Jesus' death, revealing the path to fullness (1:5). He was willing to die to himself out of love, to show a plenitude to the human soul that transcends the self. Thus, Jesus gave us the journey into the depths of our own beings, into the ground of our

[5] Walshe, *Meister Eckhart Sermons and Treatises, Volume 3*, The Talks of Instruction, 17.

own souls, "for each being has a destiny in the Transcendent Realm" (2:1).

Isaac the Syrian, speaks of this aspect of Jesus' death as a teaching for humanity: "The entire purpose of Christ's death was not to redeem us from sins, or for any other reason, but solely in order that the world might become aware of the love which God has for creation. Had all this astounding affair taken place solely for the purpose of the forgiveness of sin, it would have been sufficient to redeem us by some other means."[6]

This perspective flies in the face of later Christian orthodox belief, where Jesus' death was seen as salvific. Philip rather sees Jesus' death as iconic—thus a teaching—its deepest meanings found in the crucifixion itself, not in its theology of that event. In Jesus' death he demonstrated his primary teaching of self-denial and surrender as the ultimate act of God's love.

THE TEMPLE VEIL

The temple veil plays a significant role in this divine story. The canonical gospels tell us that at the time of Jesus' death on the cross the temple veil was split from top to bottom (eg. Matthew 27:51). Philip illuminates this text and its spiritual significance. Historically, only the temple high priest could enter beyond the veil to represent the Israelite people. Philip says that the veil was torn so that all now might have "access to the truth of hidden things" (1:6). Jesus split the veil by revealing the path of interiority to humanity. Knowledge is no longer limited to external authority, since he revealed that "the Father [God head] is there in your innermost being" (3:11). This moves human consciousness from mental

[6] Sebastian Brock, *The Wisdom of Saint Isaac the Syrian* (SLG Press, 2023), 27.

cognition to a new heart-perception in communion with the divine presence. This access and this communion are the "food" for the healing of creation, uniting all things with their divine source. It is intended that whatever is unconscious will be brought to full consciousness; an optimistic vision of creation's evolution (1:4)!

Like the naming of the temple chambers, the cardinal directions of the temple chambers—west, south, and east—are not to be taken literally, nor historically, but are implicitly metaphorical (1:2). Following ancient Jewish mystical knowledge of the four cardinal directions, they are understood as analogous and are thus spiritually iconic, revealing universal truths about these chambers of human consciousness.

Initiation into the Mysteries

> Oh, you daughters of Jerusalem, I swear to you—
> if you find my lover tell him
> I am dizzy with love! (Song of Songs 5:8)[7]

[7] *The Inclusive Bible* (Sheed and Ward, 2009). "One of the most celebrated collections of ancient love poetry, the Song of Songs—also known in English as the Song of Solomon, and referred to, by scholars, simply as the Song—is the only book of love poetry in the Bible and as such has been the subject of much speculation and controversy. For centuries, both Jewish and Christian traditions viewed the Song as spiritual allegory, thus justifying its place in the biblical canon; but this mode of interpretation, moving and imaginative as it may be, does not explain the text's primary level of meaning.... Read on the simplest level—without delving into allegory or elaborate hypotheses of structural and contextual unity—the Song reveals itself as a richly textured tapestry, woven from variegated strands of nuance and meaning. The simple level, in other words, need not be superficial; the Song is classic evidence that popular love poetry need not be slight. While it can be enjoyed solely for its surface of sensuous imagery, the Song offers even more to those who will give it a second glance, one that will more deeply pierce its skin." Marcia Falk, *The Song of Songs: A New Translation* (HarperCollins, 1990), Preface, xiii, xvii. I am bringing this love poem into our mix to show the allegorical connections with our Jewish/Christian mystical works, to be in continuity with this more ancient tradition.

The original purpose of Philip was to initiate those who were ready for the deeper life of the Spirit into these Christian mysteries:

> In our world's system there are many humans who take on animal characteristics. The wise recognize this and to swine-like beings they throw acorns. To those who are bovine in nature, they give barley, straw, and hay. To those whose characteristics are canine, bones. To servants however, they give basic fare, and to their offspring they offer complete food (5:26).

The implication is that appropriate teachings and support were offered to those in this community who demonstrated a capacity for greater understanding. Hidden teachings and suitable spiritual nurturance were given to meet the appropriate level of knowledge. When spiritual maturity was thus gained these folk were initiated into the mysteries (5:28). The first requirement was a demonstrated yearning for the life of the Spirit.

Philip says, "God created the garden of paradise and humankind dwelt there, but God's desires were not in their hearts. Their longings were elsewhere" (2:9). The whole spiritual quest is based on our hearts longings and finding its answers. At the core of this tension, we will discover that we are separated from God, and there is only one solution. When we come to recognize these innermost longings as spirit-based, it will become for us a spiritual awakening drawing us to God and to the hidden truths and mysteries of our universe. Knowing ourselves and understanding our innate longings as spiritually based is the first prerequisite to initiation into our esoteric calling and spiritual endeavor.

Philip gives us a spiritual metaphor from our genesis myth to illustrate the human condition.

> There are two trees in paradise: the one produces beasts, and the other produces humankind. It was Adam who ate from the tree producing beasts and so he himself not only became bestial but gave birth to the same (5:22).

Humans span the spectrum of consciousness. Our bodies, like all animals, have senses that bind us to the physical world—but we also have soul and access to Spirit where we can ascend to divine consciousness. At our lowest level of knowledge, we can "eat," that is, participate in animal consciousness apart from spiritual knowledge and remain beastly, even separating from God and producing evil. But we can become fully realized human beings, as well, fully at one with our creator and fully expressing the heart of God, becoming beings of love. In the book of Genesis, the tree producing beasts is called "the tree of the knowledge of good and evil," while the tree producing humans is called "the tree of life" (Genesis 2:9). Philip intends to initiate us by "feeding us" from the tree of life in order to fully live. Philip says, "Yeshua has come to us from that Realm of Truth and has brought us true food" (5:9).

Philip indicates that this initiation is only for those who are capable and prepared by the Holy Spirit to take this deeper innermost journey: "This is the way one lives into the mysteries. There is magnificence to the mystery of marital union . . . so contemplate, then, instead the union of pure spiritual embrace" (4:4). This level of contemplation requires we have a mature knowledge of life and sexuality on the physical plane in order to contemplate "pure spiritual union." This is the way one experiences the mysteries of life. We live the earthly and natural experience of our humanity, but as we become spiritually awake, are prepared for a greater spiritual undertaking of that experience, found through a deeper communion as we "enter into the presence" (1:7). For God is in all things equally. That is, God is in all aspects of our life experiences, including the sexual. All life is a manifestation of Spirit if we have the eyes to see.

Again, we hear this in Isaac the Syrian: "In love did God bring the world into existence, in love does God guide it during its temporal existence; in love is God going to bring it to that wondrous transformed state and in love will the world be swallowed up in the great mystery of God who has performed all these things. In love will the whole course of the governance of creation be finally comprised."[8]

Our initiation prepares us to see our mundane and natural world as a place alive and dynamic with the loving presence of Spirit, rather than a profane and torpid environment. When our spiritual senses are active, we then see that the earth is filled with God's glory (cf. Isaiah 6:3)! We recognize that God is present to us, even as we are reaching for God. "Truth is our Mother and knowledge of her comes through joining with her" (3:29). This is where our deep longing is drawing and opening us to God. These novices are "free," Philip says, because they have turned their back on their old self and are embracing the new reality. This is love doing its wonders because, as Philip says, love raises the hearts capacity for what is to happen (3:29).

"My lover comes to me hungry, and I to him; hungry as the deer feeding among the lilies," the poet says in Song of Songs 2:16. And then Philip tells us that the "true food"

[8] Brock, *The Wisdom of Saint Isaac the Syrian*, 31.

Jesus brought gave fullness to our lives (5:9). The food we needed was the knowledge of our own innate being and the Christian mysteries offer this spiritual insight. "Only when you have come to know your true Self will you be fully known. If, however, you never come to know who you truly are, you are a poverty-stricken being, and it is your 'self' which lies impoverished," says the Gospel of Thomas.[9] The heart comes to know before the mind what is being discovered. We only come to know ourselves as we learn to commune with the Divine Lover in our midst. This awakens the spiritual senses of the heart and opens us to spiritual energies.

> Here comes my lover, running down the mountains like a gazelle, leaping the hills like a stag in search of his doe. He is calling me: "Come, sweetheart, my pretty one, come out!" (Song of Songs 2:8-10)

Through the Sacraments

These Christian mysteries are based on our human experiences of bathing (baptism), healing our wounds (anointing), eating (Eucharist), and engaging in sexual relations (marriage)—all natural parts of being human. But the amazing discovery is that God is meeting us at every turn, waiting on our response. "Arise and come, my pretty darling, come away with me" (Song of Songs 2:13). Every rite engages the whole person, body, soul, and spirit and is experienced firstly as a very physical and sensual event, but through guidance leads us into greater knowledge and spiritual engagement. If we can perceive them correctly, these mundane, ordinary

---

[9] The Gospel of Thomas, 3, 9.

experiences are holy encounters. What before seemed common and profane we now see through the insight of these mysteries as they convey deeper knowledge and purpose to our living.

> Nothing brings you closer to God or makes God so much your own as the sweet bond of love. A person who has found this way need seek no other. Whoever hangs on this hook is caught so fast that foot and hand, mouth, eyes, and heart, and all that is theirs, belongs only to God. (Meister Eckhart)[10]

These deeper spiritual experiences are all visages of God's immanence, God's presence within. I cannot know God in any other way. I also cannot know the true quality of these experiences until I've known their spiritual foundation. Until now most of us have experienced God as totally other, completely transcendent to ourselves, but now through our new awakened consciousness we come to know God as our highest selves, closer to us than we are to our own "selves." The more we learn to live within this Presence the more God is found in the ordinariness of our lives. Paul prays for this in his letter to the Ephesians: "May Christ dwell in your hearts through faith, so that you, being rooted and grounded in love, will be able to grasp fully the breadth, length, height and depth of Christ's love and, with all God's holy ones, experience this love that surpasses all understanding, so that you may be filled with all the fullness of God" (Ephesians 3:17-19).

Baptism teaches us the depths of our lives, revealing

---

[10] Walshe, *Meister Eckhart Sermons and Treatises, Volume 1*, Sermon 4, 46.

that within the ground of our being is our true self, where we have access to Spirit in all things. The Anointing, which can heal our basic spiritual malady of separation from God, gives us the knowledge that we are not only loved by God but, in fact, are God's own precious relation, carrying forth Christ's mission.

The Eucharist gives us an awareness that our ordinary food is deeply spiritual as well as physical nurturance. Christ has been poured out for all creation and given for the life of the world. Marriage teaches us the unity of being and reveals the union of God with creation. All creation, beginning with humans, is to be brought into fullness of being, according to the unique divine expression of each thing and every individual. Creation was made for this spiritual endeavor. These mysteries are teaching us that God meets us in all aspects of our living and that all our "hungers" are ultimately a desire and need for spiritual nurturance.

Human love and sexuality bring us into a deeper human union. Spiritual love brings us into deeper communion and ultimately union with God, and the knowledge of the truth of all things. Restoration to Fullness of Being is the goal of all created things and love is the power that accomplishes it. The imbalances we currently experience—separating secular from spiritual, material from metaphysical, the natural world from humanity—are false dichotomies. We are one with the natural world because we are one with the spiritual world. Christ's Spirit binds all things in unity. It's only our mental constructs that tell us otherwise. Instead of objectifying nature we will come to unite and love her as we are coming to commune with her. God is hidden in all the many things which are portals and signs enticing and inviting us to "come and see" for God is here, waiting. The Song of Songs sings of this:

> Ah, I went looking, and found no one. But the sentries on their rounds found me, though. I wanted to ask them, 'Have you seen him, the one I love?' But no sooner did I pass by them, than I found him at last, the one that I hungered for. I put my arms around him, would not let go of him, till I had brought him home, to my mother's house, to the very room where she made me! (3:2-4)

We may have seen the world as forms of innate matter, beautiful and good, but foreign to us and unrelated, but with transformed vision we see that everything around us is animated by Spirit, drawing us ever closer to "the One in whom we live and move and have our being" (Acts 17:28). Everything is iconic, expressing its essential divine nature. In this way we know God as the essence and life of all. When our spiritual eyes are opened to the depths of all things, we come to understand that there's a spiritual relationship between us. Meister Eckhart said that when you have found this unity with God then "all things become simply God to you, for in all things you notice only God."[11]

We will also then see how in our ignorance we have impeded nature because we could not see her as divine and holy and united with us. When we are resurrected to fullness of being and our eyes are opened, we will free nature out of love. When freed to be herself, that is wild again, she will give birth to her essential goodness, manifesting her innate divine qualities. In our new resurrected state, we will innately know unity of being, for God is one.

"Some say that first the Master died and then was raised,

---

[11] Walshe, *Meister Eckhart Sermons and Treatises, Volume 1*, Sermon 4, 45.

but they are confused. First, he was resurrected, and then he died. Those who are resurrected first are like God; they are already alive and can never die" (2:6). These ancient Philip Christians understood that transcendent life is a gift to be given in this life now, in our present experience, as we are resurrected to fullness of being. This is the healing that the earth has been longing for.

Imperial Christianity put the cross of Christ at the focal point of Jesus' life, but Philip Christians put Jesus' baptism at the center. At his baptism, they understood, Jesus came into "fullness of being," which is restoration to a new life in the Spirit. Through the cross "He came to bring the system of this world to death" (3:3). The cross, they believed, demonstrated Jesus' total self-emptiness and love and stands in contradistinction to the world which esteems self-aggrandizement. Thus, the cross reveals Jesus' fullness of being, which was gained in his baptismal experience. Isaac the Syrian speaks in a similar vein:

> God surrendered God's own Son to death on the cross for the fervent love of creation.... Yet this was not because God could not redeem us in another way, but so that God's surpassing love, manifested hereby, might be a teacher unto us. And by the death of his Only-begotten Son God made us near to himself. Yes, if God had had anything more precious, God would have given it to us, so that by it our race might be God's own. Because of God's great love for us it was God's pleasure not to do violence to our freedom, but that we should draw near to God by the love of our understanding. For the sake of God's love for us and obedience to his Father,

> Christ joyfully took upon himself insult and sorrow.... In like manner, when the saints become perfect, they all attain to this perfection, and by the superabundant outpouring of their love and compassion on all, they resemble God.[12]

Jesus' inner journey exemplifies a radical shift from prayer to an external and exoteric god to contemplative prayer as silent communion with the Beloved One who dwells within. Rather than prayer being talking to God or asking something of God, it becomes—through a letting go of self-focus—an intimacy with God's Presence within, where speech is irrelevant. Jesus said, "Give attention to the Living Presence while you are alive so that when you die and have the desire to do so, you may have the power to attend."[13] This present incarnation is in continuity with our next life, one transitioning and preparing for the other.

In this silent opening to the divine presence, I leave my separate ego-focused life outside and lose myself in God. I cannot enter communion with the Beloved One and not be at one with this Reality. My highest calling is coming to know and live by the presence of the One who dwells within me, requiring a radical new shift in consciousness. A prayer that opens my heart to a new paradigm. In this deeper experience of unity of being, I discover my truest self with a greater understanding of what it means to be "God's own Child."

And here is where Philip draws the line—for this is only esoteric work and not for the uninitiated. This is solely the domain of the initiates and not for those unprepared, who

---

[12] Hilarion Alfeyev, *The Spiritual World of Isaac the Syrian* (Liturgical Press, 2000), 49.

[13] The Gospel of Thomas, 59, 26.

would misunderstand what is being taught. "If you say, 'I am the Christ,' it will indeed cause a reaction" (2:11). This is not public teaching because it is the most susceptible to misconception. The ego nullifies this deep spiritual work, because the ego cannot possibly grasp what this means since the ego itself must be transcended to come to this self-knowledge. Without a transformation of being, this work cannot possibly proceed!

CHAPTER 2
THE HOLY PLACE: BAPTISM AND ANOINTING

The first room of the temple, "which opens to the West called the Holy Place" (1:2) is a portal of coalescing, exemplified by evening, autumn, and the ingathering of the harvest, the coming together of people and a maturing state of a human being. Having gone through the physical passages of time and having been spiritually prepared and initiated into this mystical path, we are invited within, to begin the internal journey to new depths of truth, as we traverse multiple recondite spiritual stages. Having experienced the Christian mysteries on the exoteric level, we are now invited to an esoteric journey into the truth of hidden things. Jesus, according to Philip, "brought interiority into the external world, and those caught within the outer world, he took inside" (3:13).

The revelatory nature of immersion or baptism, according to Philip, can bring one into this Holy Place, where we have a new spiritual awareness of ourselves as sacred beings (1:2). The hidden or esoteric aspect of our baptism is the transcendent knowledge that "living water is itself a being" and those who come forth from those waters are "clothed with Divine Being" and "full of light" (2:18-19). External forms are simply pointing to the inner reality. The inner reality is that God is present, giving God's own self to us through the physical universe. That water is a sacred being, is knowledge we gain as we find greater unity of being, which reveals the sacredness of ourselves.

This first room, the courtyard of the Jerusalem Temple, held the altar of sacrifice and the laver for ablutions. Here in this chamber of consciousness we bring ourselves in sacrifice and are purged of the world's influence. Jesus said that if we are to follow him in discipleship we must "first deny our very selves, take up the instrument of our own death.... If you would save your life, you will lose it; but if you would lose your life for my sake, you will find it" (Matthew 16:24-25). The ego is anathema to this deep spiritual work of transformation. To follow Jesus into this inner path, we must first turn our backs on what we thought was our very self, as we learn it is our "false self."

The outer form of baptism, if seen from the esoteric viewpoint, opens us into a new life in the Spirit, into what Philip calls Resurrection. This is the beginning of a new transformation of us as our spiritual work is beginning to make the external persona more consonant with the innermost being, as we are becoming single and whole, and not divided. Our essential self is becoming more manifest and fully realized. In our anointing, at our baptisms, we receive a deeper knowledge of our true self as a being of light. With this new knowledge we experience ourselves not only as physical beings, but more truly amphibious, at home in both worlds.

Paul speaks to this in his letter to the Ephesians: "You must give up your old way of life; you must put aside your old self, which is being corrupted by following illusory desires. Your mind must be renewed by a spiritual revolution, so that you can put on the new self that has been created in God's likeness, in the justice and holiness of the truth" (Ephesians 4:22-24).

"It is imperative," according to Philip, "that one not be reborn in symbol only" (2:8). These mysteries point beyond the superficial experience to the in-depth spiritual—where we experience what Jesus called our conversion of life: "change your hearts and minds" (Mark 1:14-15). We might say that this is a reversal of consciousness, moving our locus of perception from mental cognition to intuitive heart-knowledge. In the New Testament Greek, this change in consciousness, *metanoia*, speaks of going beyond our normal consciousness (*nous*), to a new apperception (*meta*), a heart sensitivity. This happens as we are becoming more aware of the presence of God.

New forms of prayer and reflection are also being sought and found. Our spirit is hungry for the life of the spirit and we are increasingly opening to that life. "Praise to You Beloved who became for us the Mediator for these good things, through whom we have been held worthy to receive, know, and perceive in faith 'what eye has not seen, ear has not heard,' [1 Corinthians 2:9] nor have the senses of the soul been able to conceive concerning these good things that God has now brought out into the open in these 'First-fruits' from us." (Isaac the Syrian)[1]

THE WORK OF DISCERNMENT

In this first stage of new awareness, we see the world more holistically, unified, and balanced—the "union of opposites," according to Philip. Philip 3:8 speaks of the confusion of humanity, unable to read the physical world, confounding its transcendent and immanent aspects. This includes not truly knowing ourselves, confusing our egotistical state, which is temporal, with our transcendent state, which is eternal (3:6). In this incomplete and immature state, we are

[1] Brock, *Headings on Spiritual Knowledge*, 102.

not whole beings, the inner (consciousness) and the outer (physical and mental) aspects are split, causing us to be divided and not whole. Jesus said, "If you become whole you will be full of Light. If you remain fragmented darkness will fill you."[2] Philip sadly reminds us that, "Anyone unreceptive to the transcendent continues on in lower realities" (3:33). The lower realities being where most humans seem to be "caught" until freed by this interior path. "It is entirely fitting for that which is below to move upward to that which is above" (1:4).

Many of us are deceived, and "not able to recognize our true reality," which is, "a natural kinship to that which is truly good" (5:13). This may come as a shock to orthodox Christians who have been taught that human nature is intrinsically flawed and basically evil. Not so, according to these more ancient Christians. God has created us in the divine image. For Philip, this first level of transcendence awakens us to this reality, with a knowledge of ourselves as God's beloved children. As we learn to let go of old concepts of ourselves, we simultaneously rebirth in God. We are being brought, through this rebirth, to full maturity, to being fully realized as God (3:26), for "God gives birth to God" (4:11).

We will feel a disparity between our physical self and our spiritual identity and thus begins the journey to our unity of being. Again, Symeon the New Theologian speaks of this experience within himself:

> You became one with me; no division, indeed, between Your essential faculties, no separation, Your nature is Your essence and Your essence your nature. Thus, uniting with Your body, I

[2] The Gospel of Thomas, 61, 27.

> participate in Your nature and I really take as mine a part of your essence, uniting with your divinity, much more becoming heir in my body, I become son of God as You have said, not for the angels, but for us, calling us gods in these terms: "I have said: You are all gods and sons of the Most High." Glory be to Your mercy and to Your Divine Plan, because You became human, You who by nature are God...have made me, a mortal by my nature, a god, god by adoption, god by Your grace, by power of Your Spirit, uniting miraculously, God that You are, the two extremes.[3]

"It is important," Philip says, "that the interior and the exterior exist together beyond all externals." In other words, we are to come to a spiritual "coalescing," which can only happen in a transcendent state. The Gospel of Thomas quotes Jesus as talking about this issue with his disciples:

> Yeshua noticed an infant nursing and said to his students, "These little ones taking milk are like those on their way into the kingdom." So they asked him, "If we too are 'little ones' are we on our way into the kingdom?" Yeshua replied,
> "When you are able to make two become one, the inside like the outside, and the outside like the inside, the higher like the lower, so that a man is no longer male, and a woman, female, but male and female become a single whole. When you are able to fashion an eye to replace an eye, and form a hand in place of a hand, or

[3] Maloney, *Saint Symeon the New Theologian*, Hymn 7, 193.

> a foot for a foot, making one image supersede another—then you will enter in."[4]

This stage of spiritual work requires a sorting out and a clarification of what is real and what is only a manifestation of the real. It is marked by an intense time of discernment. Humans often have worshipped and put too much trust in that which is neither real nor essential. In this transition we are learning to discern the difference, and this first portal, the "holy place," holds a key to the greater truths lying within us, beyond the external forms. We are seeing the truth of our essential selves. Our old identities no longer hold, as we open to new spiritual possibilities. When prepared, guided by the Holy Spirit and having gone through a purification process, we can go further into depths of knowledge.

The immensity of this new inner work brings us more intensely to the work of discernment and the knowledge of God's will at one with our own. This requires a turning from external forms of authority and finding that authority within, "for the Son of Humanity already exists within you," which is exemplified by a "peace residing within" me.[5] Peace is a sign that we are in unity of being, at one with Christ.

JESUS' BAPTISM

Jesus experienced this new reality in an enlightening experience at his baptism, according to Philip. Jesus wasn't born enlightened but he was given enlightenment, as all humans must, through the experience of unity with God. As we can, he "learned to obey through suffering" (Hebrews 5:8). But

[4] The Gospel of Thomas, 22, 17.

[5] The Dialogues of Mary Magdalene, Dialogue 1, 66.

in his baptism he had a vision in which the veil between his physical world and the spiritual world was removed giving him an imminent experience of God (cf. Matthew 3:16). It was an experience of deep self-knowledge, confirming his life's mission. According to Philip, this was Jesus' christening and from this moment on he was "the Christ," "the one consecrated to God" (2:5). In this experience, Philip tells us, he also received "resurrection," (new spiritual life), "its light," (enlightenment), "its cross," (his mission), "its Sacred Spirit," (unity with God) (2:12).

His baptism was also a revelation of God's purpose for all humanity. "At the river Jordan Yeshua revealed the great fullness that is the Kingdom of the Heavens, which existed before all things" (5:1). "So let us speak then of this great mystery in this way: The Father of All came down and united with the virgin, and on that day made light shine forth from the fire—revealing to us the power of the Bridal Chamber" (5:2). Before the universe was created in multiplicity there was simply One. And now through his baptism Jesus reveals that a return to "One-ness of being" is creation's purpose and goal. "When you are able to make two become One... then you will enter in."[6]

When Philip speaks of "the virgin" here it is understood metaphorically. In 4:5 it says, "Let not the Bridal Chamber be for animals, slaves, or harlots. Rather let it be for those both free and virginal." This term "virgin" refers to those who taking this inner journey, have turned their backs on their animalistic-egotistical selves, and are no longer slaves to the world and its systems. Now, guided by the Spirit, they're open to greater spiritual perception, freed of self-focus and the cultural chains, and are thus virginal and prepared to

---

[6] The Gospel of Thomas, 22, 17.

receive the "hidden truths." Jesus said, "If you do not fast from the cosmos, you will never grasp Reality."[7]

This first chamber is a place of sacrifice. Jesus said that if we desire to follow him in discipleship the first requirement is self-denial. Laying aside our self-aggrandizement we are then able to follow him into the inner chambers where communion with God is possible.

Meister Eckhart said Jesus was "empty and free and virginal in himself, offering no hindrance to the highest Truth. Since union comes only by the joining of like to like, therefore they must be a virgin who would receive God's most beloved will."[8] Eckhart takes us into this mystery, as Philip does, for he says: "Now attend and follow me closely. If a person were to be ever virginal, they would bear no fruit. If a person is to be fruitful, they must be a wife. 'Wife' is the noblest title one can bestow on the soul—far nobler than 'virgin.' But for God to be fuitful in that person it is better...and herein the spirit is a wife...bearing Jesus again in God's paternal heart."[9]

During Jesus' baptism he experienced unity with the Godhead ("father of all"), and was thus "restored to fullness of being,"— "a bridegroom with his bride" (5:2). Jesus being virginal was capable and ready for sacred marriage. In the letter to the Philippians, we are told that Jesus "emptied himself" (Philippians 2:7), that is, became empty of self, turning his back on his own self-interests. His experience revealed the path to inner realities for all of us who would follow him into "this hidden place within" (3:11).

Resurrection, according to Philip, is meant to be a present spiritual reality because of our baptisms, which are icons revealing to us hidden realities. "Those who go down

[7] The Gospel of Thomas, 27, 18.
[8] Walshe, *Meister Eckhart Sermons and Treatises, Volume 1*, Sermon 8, 71.
[9] Walshe, *Meister Eckhart Sermons and Treatises, Volume 1*, Sermon 8, 72.

into the waters of baptism are not immersed into death but brought forth into the great restoration" (2:22). "Those who say that they will die and then be raised are confused. If while still alive they do not first enter the resurrection, they will receive nothing when they die" (3:23). This point is a huge emphasis in this ancient Gospel. Salvation, i.e., unity with God, is a present earthly experience, not something for a future state. This answers why we are in this earth journey through time. It is here, only in this place, that we are united with God, so we "may never die" (5:9). For Jesus this meant he became the Christ, the God-bearer, to heal a broken and lost humanity. Philip takes great umbrage with those who would say that salvation is given when we get to heaven, after death. This Gospel is emphatic that we are here, now, to come to know God, who is already present with us. However, Philip warns, we cannot even perceive of such a thing until we "possess it" (2:2).

The author of Philip emphasizes this point because there was apparent controversy concerning the issue of resurrection and its implications for salvation. Interjecting a rare personal opinion into the text the author says, "I oppose those who deny that neither form nor flesh shall rise from the dead" (2:26). The author goes on to argue that since all things arise through some form of incarnation, then both sacred body ("Light enfleshed") and the spirit, being holy, will rise to new life, which cannot die. The point is again emphasized that those who are in communion, that is union with the divine Life, cannot die, but have already risen from the mere physical realm and are transcendent beings here on earth. Through Spirit the physical body is also divinized.

> It is crucial, then, to become fully realized before moving beyond this world. Whoever

> receives this gift without achieving mastery in this domain will have no mastery in any other, moving forward through these transitions in an imperfect state. Only Yeshua knows what the destiny of such a person will be (3:19).

THE ANOINTING

"The oil of anointing," Philip says, "is superior to the waters of immersion, for because of the anointing we too are also called 'the Christ' just as Yeshua was" (2:12). The anointing, at our baptisms, opens us to the knowledge of our transcendent state: "Sons and Daughters of The Human One," i.e., "True Humanity" (4:11). "Fire is hidden in the oil of anointing," Philip reveals—a presence that ultimately purifies us entirely (2:29-30) for "God is a consuming fire" (Hebrews 12:29). As Symeon the New Theologian echoed: "I am filled with God's love and God's beauty, and I am sated with divine delight and sweetness. I share in the light, I participate also in the glory, and my face shines like my Beloved's, and all my members become bearers of light...for I possess the Creator of the whole universe."[10]

At our baptism we are given chrismation marking us as "Christ's own forever." This baptism and chrismation reveal what is to happen as we mature in Christ. This is the direct route to our highest self-knowledge. Our anointing carries immense power, according to Philip, in that we like Jesus are set aside at our baptisms for this transcendent experience of coming into full unity with God, revealing to us what it means to be "God's own, God's Beloved" (Matthew 3:17).

In our present conscious state, we cannot know, nor

[10] Maloney, *Saint Symeon the New Theologian*, Hymn 16, 222.

can we imagine what this means. This knowledge of ourselves as God's children is to be brought to fruition as we become fully realized human beings. "It is good to call the offspring who have been chosen by the Sacred Spirit, the 'True Humanity' and 'Sons and Daughters of the Human One.'... This new race bears the name 'True Human' in this world, and it is here in this very place, where they become the sons and daughters" (4:11).

The quest for self-knowledge directly depends on our knowledge of God. This knowledge is gained only in the unitive experience; with a perception from the inside, where we come to see as God sees. "Should you come to see yourself in that realm beyond this world, you would become what you see" (3:4). This transcendent knowledge unites our image to the archetype, "Perfect Light with Sacred Spirit" (3:10). Philip tells us that Jesus revealed himself to others "according to the capacities "of the observers. And goes on, "though some who saw him realized they were seeing themselves" (3:9). Self-knowledge is the highest form of spiritual knowledge and our true enlightened state!

Jesus experienced this enlightenment at his baptism when the veil between earth and heaven was rent, and he received the knowledge that "This is my Own, my Beloved, on whom my favor rests" (Matthew 3:17). To be given this profound knowledge of ourselves is the wisdom needed for our transformation and wholeness. "To see one's true self, it is necessary to be immersed in both—the light as well as the water, and the light is present in the oil of anointing" (3:5). This "Light" is enlightenment and comes as we find greater unity with God; giving us a new identity, with the knowledge of ourselves as beings who carry divine DNA. "All those who confirm, 'I am the Christ,' also come from that transcendent place beyond confusion" (2:9). This insight is given by the Holy Spirit who reveals our essential nature to us (3:6). We are clothed with Light; that is clothed with our spiritual body revealing our intrinsic identity, as "that which is Truly Good" and of Divine essence.

"The Christ" or the Anointed One, Philip tells us, is "Messiah" in Aramaic (2:5). We too become the Christ, we thus help fulfill that messianic mission. This is knowledge that is necessary as we come to know who we are and what that means for the created order. The Messiah isn't coming from outside of ourselves to intervene in human history and destiny. Rather this coming happens as we are given our truest self-knowledge. This is the initiation necessary concerning our baptisms and anointing for "we too are also called 'the Christ,'" the Messiah, carrying that responsibility to fulfill Christ's mission restoring all things as the creator intended (2:8). Bringing the earth back into wholeness can only happen when humanity itself discovers the "truth of hidden things" (1:7). Until we have come into our resurrected and perfected state creation itself cannot be completed because God needs humankind to finish the creation.

THE ICONIC NATURE OF THE UNIVERSE

The acquisition of truth is primary to the Gospel of Philip. Philip's epistemology is "Truth did not come to us in this world naked. Rather it was clothed with symbol and image, for it cannot be received in any other way" (2:8)—for, indeed, the only means by which humans grasp truth begins on the surface of life, with what can be perceived by our physical senses, and what we can name and understand with our mental capacity.

The outer forms, if understood appropriately as iconic, would teach us the transcendent truth of their essential nature. Awakening to the reality that all "things" function this way—pointing beyond themselves—our senses receive fuller knowledge of our state of being. The enlightened soul can perceive "beyond confusion" what the mind cannot possibly grasp (2:9). Enlightenment, according to Philip, is one of the primary elements that God uses to cultivate and "ripen" humankind and restore the earth (5:32). Jesus himself is the icon of icons: "As the Anointed One, he contains everything within his heart: the human, the archetype, the mystery, and the Father" (2:5).

Here Philip is laying out the great cosmic secret, and the clue to the mystery of creation itself. These symbols and images are pointing to and teaching us about the core and essence of our cosmos. This is our path to knowledge. External appearances are simply allegories of profounder depths. In other words, the universe is a great poem, sung into being by the Creator.

These external manifestations are guides and teachings, if only we have the eyes to see and the ears to hear, "for everything rises through some form of incarnation, for everything is held there in its very heart" (2:26). Everything and everybody is reflecting its divine archetype. The many things are teaching us the great unity: revealing the Creator, declaring God as the ground of all being (2:3). Words alone cannot teach us, and often they fail in leading us. Philip is telling us that the universe itself, "the many things," is a great metaphor that helps our limited minds and souls awaken to the great reality at the core of this poetic revelation. God's language is silence, but humans need metaphor and icons to lead us to the greater language of God, where we are learning to hear without mediation.

Humans are created in the divine image, according to Philip (cf. Genesis 1:27). Philip adds to this that we are not real until we've been united to our archetype, the Christ. Jesus prayed, according to Philip, "come bind our Angels (Archetypes) to the icons" (3:10). Oneness with the Creator was Jesus' nobility. It was also the point of this prayer, that his students also might participate in this reality, and thus become fully realized human beings as he was. Until we have participated in this unity of being, there can be no fruitfulness. We cannot love as God loves, we cannot speak the words of God, we cannot steward and cultivate the earth until God is born in us and we have become the Christ. Again, Symeon the New Theologian echoes this:

> Possess the work of faith, the confirmation of faith and the seal of faith and the perfection of faith without ambivalence, from the fact that you have put on Christ consciously and knowingly who radiates, is resplendent in the glory of the divinity and who in a light most clear completely transforms you, leaving you...god by adoption and completely human by nature.[11]

All of this means ultimate truth is not found at the literal or surface level in our Christian rites, in the reading of Scripture, or in deciphering of nature. The world is iconic as are words, and like all great poetry, point beyond themselves to a deeper meaning found within, layer upon layer, as our imaginations are opened to greater and more complex knowledge, for "it cannot be received in any other way" (2:8). As Jesus said, "What your own eyes cannot see, your human ears do not hear, your physical hands cannot touch, and what is inconceivable to the human mind—that I will

[11] Maloney, *Saint Symeon the New Theologian*, Hymn 52, 433.

give you!"[12] The Spirit is given to us to "lead us into all truth" (John 16:13) because we need guidance and enlightenment to comprehend the reality of the truth of our lives.

Philip tells us that Jesus was an icon of God, but people could only know and understand him according to their spiritual capacity. "To the great ones he revealed himself as great; to the little ones he became small. To angels he revealed himself as angel, to humanity as a man. Yet in all of these the Logos itself was the hidden secret, though some who saw him realized they were seeing themselves" (3:9). Grasping who Jesus was, was according to the capability of the observer. However, all external observances were short of a full revelation of who Jesus truly was. To see his nobility as the Logos, the Word of God being spoken, it was necessary to have spiritual perception.

When transcendent perception is given, we will not only know the deep mystery of who Jesus is but will understand ourselves through the same light (3:9). This is how Philip understands all of creation, since all things are incarnational the ground of all things is the Logos. Like the Temple, there is the outer physical form, inviting us within, and then there are chambers of experience but the Holy of Holies, the innermost chamber, or the heart of a human being alone can perceive the mystery of God who is present.

> At present we are surrounded by the visible manifestations of creation. Some call these strong and valuable, while what is unseen or unknown is deemed weak and contemptible. The truth is, however, that what is manifest is

[12] The Gospel of Thomas, 17, 14.

> weak and inferior, while what is unseen is powerful and praiseworthy (4:2).

In fact, Philip says that "it is not possible for a person to see the higher realities of existence unless that person has become as real as they are" (3:4). As we commune—spirit to spirit—we will see ourselves at one with the world and understand the other by kinship with our own being. All creatures are one in being, therefore there is a knowledge by relationship and communion with the presence of God is the essential quality that changes our perception of all things and opens us to their inner meaning. This requires a self-forgetfulness that simultaneously opens our attentiveness and allows us to concentrate and commune by way of self-merging. This "becoming what we are perceiving" gives us the knowledge of the Spirit in all things.

ABANDONING OLD CONCEPTS

Contemplation gives us a power of perception opening us to divine reality: a "transcendent place beyond confusion" of the natural mind (2:9). Meister Eckhart reinforces Philip on this subject:

> You have to be and dwell in the essence and in the ground, and *there* God will touch you with God's simple essence without the intervention of any image. No image represents and signifies itself: it always aims and points to that of which it is the image. And therefore there must be a silence and a stillness, and the Father must speak in that.[13]

[13] Walshe, *Meister Eckhart Sermons and Treatises, Volume 1*, Sermon 1, 6.

Like the clothes we wear or language we speak, symbols can hide greater insight, or the essential nature, which must be uncovered to find the truth within. "On the day you strip yourselves naked...and take your clothes and trample them on the ground under your feet without shame, then you will be able to look upon the son of the Living One without fear."[14] This is primarily speaking of our old persona, which must be abandoned for a truer self-knowledge. But these clothes can also be speaking of the external perceptions of all things. These external "clothes" act as guides and point us to greater truths beyond themselves. And then these icons will ultimately have to be abandoned for the greater truths to be grasped.

Concerning ourselves, we will have to abandon all old concepts of who we are—our ego-based personas—in order to see our essential self, "the [child] of the Living One," that we are coming to see! This, Philip says, is the purpose of our baptisms, "in order that the spirit of this world might be poured away from us" (2:20).

Philip also says that out of ignorance we have attempted to name the transcendent realm, such as "God, Father, Son, Holy Spirit, life, light, resurrection and church"—but these names are illusory, based on mental constructs (2:1). Our attempts through rationality to name the transcendent fails because our consciousness has not reached its depth of being. Not knowing God, through unity of being, our ideas of God and things spiritual are limited to empirical knowledge which is incapable of transcendent knowledge. When we begin to shift our focus from that of the small mind to heart awareness—allowing us to see as God sees from the inside out—we

[14] The Gospel of Thomas, 37, 20.

will begin to have a God-centric viewpoint, which is therefore earth-centered, other-centered.

All we can conceive of God and the natural world through empirical knowledge causes us to anthropomorphize God and the natural world as we perceive it, which leads then into deeper errors. In most cases, our names for God are based on human patriarchal or societal concepts. These appellations are created by our imaginations in attempts to make sense of the transcendent. Instead, note that when Moses encountered the burning bush on Mt. Horeb, he asked God's name and was told, "I AM WHO I AM" (Exodus 3), or perhaps more correctly translated, "I WILL BE WHAT I WILL BE."[15] In other words, God isn't named but experienced. God is a verb and not a noun. God is the active agent in the lives of our ancestors and in our lives today.

God will be whatever we experience God to be in our own lives. That's who God is and why we need to free God within us to be active. We can only know God through God's actions in us. As Meister Eckhart said, we need to "leave God for God" in order to know God as "God is essentially in Godself."[16] In other words, we need to detach from all concepts of God in order to come to an immanent experiential knowledge of God. Truth is not an objective formula or law. Truth is not contained in books and creeds. The truth of our lives is present and active in the here and now, in this very present moment, in these circumstances, in this ephemeral encounter with God.

According to Philip, God cannot be known by mental

---

[15] Lawrence Kushner, *Eyes Remade for Wonder* (Jewish Lights Publishing, 1998), 144.

[16] Walshe, *Meister Eckhart Sermons and Treatises, Volume 2*, Sermon 57, 85.

cognition at all. God can only be known as we come into a new transcendent state experienced through spiritual baptism (our resurrection into wholeness of being), where we have spiritually assimilated into the Real. Philip gives us a mystical story to explain the esoteric experience of our baptisms:

> The Master went into the dye works of Levi and took seventy-two colors and threw them into a vat, but then what he drew up out of it was entirely white.[17] "This," he said, "is the way in which the Son of Humanity comes to you as a dyer" (2:16).

We are emersed in the spiritual vat of divinity and permanently saturated with God's essence as we are baptized spiritually. When our essential being and our outer countenance become one in wholeness: "the inside like the outside, and the outside like the inside, the higher like the lower."[18] Then the split in our nature is healed. "It is in this way that he completes the right-relationship between all things" (2:22). We "become as real" as God is (3:4).

---

[17] This passage points to aspects of Jewish mysticism. The number 72 often refers to the 72 names of God, as found by Jewish mystics in Exodus 14:19-21, where Moses parted the Red Sea. The color white is, of course, all colors combined, inferring that what God does is clothe us with God's own characteristics. Much mystical knowledge is embedded in this story and could be spiritually discerned.

[18] The Gospel of Thomas, 22, 17.

CHAPTER 3

THE HOLY OF HOLIES: EUCHARIST

The second chamber of the Mystical Temple "opens to the South and is," called by Philip, "the Holy of Holies" (1:2)—a place of greater lucidity. To go there requires a movement of even deeper interiority where the outer forms of religion are left behind and the teachings of childhood are abandoned for a maturity of faith and clarity of purpose—for a life given to love. This teaching initiates us into the higher stages of spiritual maturation and knowledge: the reign of love.

This second chamber of the Jerusalem Temple held three primary objects: the altar of incense, ten golden candlesticks, and the Bread of the Presence. The incense communicated that this was a place of prayer. The ten golden candlesticks represented knowledge of God. The Bread of Presence spoke of the presence of God within the material realms, offering physical and spiritual nurturance.

The Eucharistic "cup is filled with Spirit, which is for the perfecting of humanity. Whoever drinks from the cup becomes a completed being" (3:1). Philip is, of course, speaking metaphorically. Drinking from the cup is participation in the divine life. Whoever is living in communion with Jesus' blood, that is, his life, will inherit God's kingdom (2:27). A completed being is a person in balance, at One with God, living fully in both worlds: the physical as well as the spiritual. The Eucharist reveals to us the presence of Spirit in our lives. God comes to us through the material realm, uniting us with the spiritual.

Eucharist gives us the knowledge that God is one in all things and received through all things, first experiencing God feeding us through food and drink. We increasingly embrace that presence, encountering God in all things and in all beings equally. Our knowledge of each other also comes by way of this communion with God. Unity experienced in communion unites us with Spirit in all things, and these encounters draw us ever closer into unity with the Beloved. In proportion to our spiritual unity, we will increasingly manifest God's goodness, beauty, and truth in our lives thus making that hidden presence known. "Yeshua is the Eucharistic feast, because in Aramaic he is called *farisatha*—the One opened out and extended over all," Philip explains (3:3), perhaps echoing St. Paul: "There is only Christ, who is all, and in all" (Colossians 3:11).

CONTEMPLATIVE PRAYER

Moving into this second chamber, called by Philip "Restoration to Fullness of Being," involves a further and deeper step into contemplative prayer—a new conscious awareness of the presence of God permeating my being, as I am silent, still, and detached from all that is not God. Letting go of my obsessive self-focus and turning to the chambers within, a new fuller awareness emerges. We hear roots of these mysteries in the ancient Song of Songs:

> I enter your garden, my sister-bride, to gather myrrh and spice. I eat of your honeycomb, and drink honeyed wine with sweet milk.
>
> *Eat, friends, and drink!*

Sate yourself, oh lovers. (5:1)

This also connects me most directly with Jesus' primary teaching on discipleship, "If any of you come to me without turning your back on your mother and your father, your loved ones, your sisters and brothers, indeed your very self, you can't be my follower. Anyone who doesn't take up their cross and follow me can't be my disciple" (Luke 14:25-26). This involves a spiritual transformation for humanity, making an almost impossible demand upon us. Jesus said, "I tell you this, whoever of you becomes 'a little child' will not only know the kingdom but will be raised to a state higher than John's."[1] This state that is to be raised "higher than John's" is speaking of our present conscious spiritual condition, which too must be transcended. Becoming "a little child" speaks of a disassociation from old identities and personas that we have previously identified with, but are now coming to see, are not our essential selves. Jesus is asking us to become open, vulnerable, and real about who we are and what is authentic in order to become a true student, following him.

Becoming a little child is also the ontological condition of self-emptiness (*kenosis*). It is the prerequisite necessary to finding our fullness (*pleroma*) in God. "All who are empty shall be filled" (4:33). Emptiness is the prerequisite for spiritual knowledge. Our part is learning to detach in order to become open and free, no longer clinging to ideas and dogmas or self-aggrandizement. It means I relinquish my self-centeredness and willingly sacrifice my own self in order to become a servant to the reign of God. It also means letting go of all concepts of God, trusting our transformation

[1] The Gospel of Thomas, 46, 22.

to our Creator when we have been made ready by becoming a little child again.

This detachment means most importantly being willing to not know, accepting the condition of unknowing. That is, not clinging to our ideas and viewpoints, and especially theological notions. Unknowing is the hardest condition because we have been conditioned to believe that clinging to what we think we know is being faithful, but it is the opposite. It is an egotistical stance based on a belief that I can know something spiritually on the sensual and cognitive level. But we are in fact clinging to what we in fact do not know. This is why emptiness is the ontological condition necessary for God's fullness in our lives. Our capacity for spiritual "knowledge" depends upon our degree of emptiness. We must come to a place where we are outside of our mental processes and attentive to the stillness of the heart. Only in silence and emptiness are we made capable of God-receptivity.

The vision Philip holds for us is a path of transformation. The goal is not more information or more theology or a new belief system, nor a perfect life, but a complete change in our conscious awareness. Jesus said in the Gospel of Thomas, "If you come to know all, and yet you yourself are lacking, you have missed everything."[2] This path Jesus gives his followers is the most arduous a human can make. But leaving the self-focus and the external knowledge behind brings about a necessary state of virginity and openness to God that is transformative. "Should you come to see yourself in that realm beyond this world, you would become what you see" (3:4). We will never come to understand who we are until we've seen and known Jesus as the Christ and what his

---

[2] The Gospel of Thomas, 67, 30.

essential being represents as the fully realized human, "for some who saw him realized they were seeing themselves" (3:9). Our capacity to "see" spiritually is made possible by the "eyes of the heart."

Again, as Jesus said in the Gospel of Thomas:

> What your own eyes cannot see, your human ears do not hear, your physical hands cannot touch, and what is inconceivable to the human mind—that I will give to you![3]

Philip tells us that Jesus "took everyone by surprise, for he did not reveal himself as he truly was, but only according to the capacities of those who were able to perceive him" (3:9). In other words, the truth of who Jesus was and is, cannot be found by holding onto theological positions or creeds, but as the Spirit opens our spiritual eyes in understanding. When Jesus asked his disciples, "Who do you say that I am?" Simon Peter answered, "You are the Messiah, the Firstborn of the Living God!" Jesus replied, "Blessed are you, Simon ben-Jonah! No mere mortal has revealed this to you, but my Abba God in heaven" (Matthew 16:15-16). Spiritual knowledge will come to us, not through human concepts, but as we are taught by God!

WORK OF THE HEART

This evolving perspicacity comes solely by way of the heart, as "you yourself are transcending toward matters of truth" (3:4), "not obvious to the naked eye" (5:29). This is a revelation of Christ which simultaneously gives us new self-knowledge.

---

[3] The Gospel of Thomas, 17, 14.

An insight revealing the truth of Jesus the Christ as archetype of our anthropic condition—my condition. I now see myself through the icon of the first "fully realized human being," revealing who I, in this transcendent state, am as well. Jesus said to his disciples, "When the time comes that you are able to look upon the icon of your own being which came into existence at the beginning, and neither dies nor has been fully revealed, will you be able to stand it?"[4] He's inviting his disciples to prepare through self-emptiness for a fuller, richer self-knowledge.

Those few who when seeing the Christ "realized they were seeing themselves," are those who in self-abandonment and communion are brought into unity of being. It's the spiritual goal and ultimate human perception. It answers Jesus' final words of instructions as told by John, "A little while now and the world will see me no more; but you'll see me; because I live, and you will live as well. On that day you'll know that I am in God, and you are in me, and I am in you" (John 14:19-20). There is only one being, and that being is God. We are brought into being and fullness as we are united to God.

And here, Philip points to our most sensitive inner work, based on our heart's receptivity:

> Those to whom Truth is given no longer offend, so the world calls them "free!" They cease their transgressions because they have gained wisdom from truth, which raises the level of their hearts, and having transcended their state in the world, they are free indeed. Love, however, is what uplifts and frees them" (3:29).

[4] The Gospel of Thomas, 84, 34.

Freedom is the goal of all spiritual work, and the knowledge and wisdom gained through our communion with God will set us on its course.

Without love that binds us to God and God to us, this work cannot happen. Freedom from bondage to our cultures, to our biased and cultivated thinking, to our habits and addictions, is the concerns of all spiritual work. To be free is to be released from all constrictions, particularly mental stenosis. Listen to the Gospel of Philip:

> Those who gain wisdom from truth are liberated beings, and a liberated being is one who does not habitually transgress—transgressors being slaves of their own offenses. Truth is our Mother and knowledge of her comes through joining with her. Those to whom Truth is given no longer offend, so the world calls them "free!" They cease their transgressions because they have gained wisdom from Truth, which raises the level of their hearts, and having transcended their state in the world, they are free indeed. (3:29)

Freedom is the absence of obstacles and is empty. It's like an open road where nothing blocks the way. This is why the initial work is to detach from self-focus and the mind's constructs. The New Testament calls this, in Jesus, *kenosis*—self-emptying (Philippians 2:5). When we are no longer occupied by constant self-focus and humbled, our obstructions to greater transcendence are cleared. We've opened the path to unity with God.

Freedom is humanity's greatest gift, but the one most

squandered. Jesus removed the veil that prevents us from access to this most holy place, where God is met, welcoming our homecoming. St. Paul said as much:

> But whenever anyone turns to Our God, the veil is removed. Now Our God is the Spirit, and where the Spirit of Our God is, there is freedom. And we, who with unveiled faces reflect Our God's glory, grow brighter and brighter as we are being transformed into the image we reflect. This is the work of Our God, who is Spirit. (2 Corinthians 3:16-18)

This new state of consciousness comes from unity of being, "joining with Truth" through love "transcending their state in the world." Love is not an emotion here, but the act of re-orienting the soul toward our deepest truth and the ground of being, where God is present with us. This is where our hunger meets God's love and in communion we find unity. This new consciousness will raise our capacity for greater love and compassion toward all things and all people. It makes us conscious lovers with a deep knowledge of who and what we are. It gives us new eyes to perceive the world in which we live; new hands to do the work of the Spirit in the world. Through this inner work, I am a new, fully realized human being, the Christ, and begin to come to know myself from a divine perspective.

THE PRAYER OF THE HEART

The Gospel of Philip encourages us in our pursuit of truth. For Jesus, enlightenment seems to have been a singular ecstatic experience, but for most of us it comes incrementally.

"What you see from beyond comes because you yourself are transcending towards them," Philip says (3:4). It's a process of becoming enlightened, that is, becoming more and more attuned to "the One who is in this hidden place within you" (3:11). For Philip, it's a matter of diligence with the soul's sojourn into the depths of being. It's a movement of conscious awareness from mental cognition to the heart's knowing. Moving our center of cognition to the heart where we discover new spiritual perceptivity.

Using the same quote from Jesus' prime teachings on prayer found in the Gospel of Matthew 6:6, Philip quotes Jesus: "My Father dwells in secret, so go into the hidden chamber and shut the door and commune there with the One who is in this hidden place within you." Then Philip explains: "The Father is there in your innermost being, and there is no other place transcendent to this, which is the Fullness beyond all 'place'" (3:11).

In other words, the path to God does not come by way of escaping the physical, but by going deeply within it, as we transcend "ourselves." Selfhood dies and is reborn in God. And is the reason we are invited by Jesus into the "holiest of holy places," the innermost chamber of ourselves, where God resides as the ground of our own being.

This "prayer of the heart," as it was called by later monastics, is front and center for Philip. It is the direct path to transformation as we're drawn into deeper communion with the presence of God within. As we practice and learn to live with this presence, we come into greater unity with the Spirit who is in all, desiring to work through all. It begins as practice but ends as a state of being.

Shush, shush—
come here, my love,

> fast, like the gazelle—
> be like a young stag
> on these mountains of spice.
> (Song of Songs 8:14)

A necessary component to this contemplative prayer-work is to "shut the door" on the outside world to maintain purity of purpose while seeking unity with that presence. "Do not take your possessions into it, and do not remove anything from it," Philip quotes Jesus (3:12).

This prayer must be guarded and kept untainted. It is the most sacred and holy act we can make. We can only enter this innermost chamber when we're fully in the present without distractions. It requires our complete vigilance! But ultimately this practice will, in Philip's words, "restore us to fullness of being" (2:9), as we "become fully realized human beings as well as the Logos" (5:5).

"When the Anointed One came, he brought interiority into the external world, and those caught within the outer world, he took inside" (3:13). Communing with the One hidden within, then, is the secret to coming to this essential knowledge of truth. Not an "external place," not an intellectual pursuit, but a journey of soul to the silent stillness of the heart. Now we discover that the highest truths are perceived by way of the heart. And we experience ourselves as microcosms of the universe where at the core of our being dwells the One who holds it all together, the ancient *Shekinah* of the inner-most Temple, welcoming our discovery.

"The soul—a precious thing—has come to exist in a humble body" (2:31). What happens to the human soul (that is, consciousness) is the crux of the matter. Meister Eckhart also speaks of the soul's purpose:

> When God creates the soul, God creates the soul and begats God's only-begotten Son into the soul, at the same time and above time: thus God pours God's image into the soul.[5]

This is the ground where God works when we are free, open, and virginal. In this work, God is birthing God's child through us as we are "formed anew in the image of our Creator. And in that image, there is no Greek or Hebrew; no Jew or Gentile, no barbarian or Scythian; no slave or citizen, no male or female (Galatians 3:28). There is only Christ, who is "all and in all" (Colossians 3:11).

In another portion of Philip, talking about the spiritual needs of individuals, it says, "If [these teachers] are wise and truly understand the principle of discipleship they will perceive the inner condition of each individual's soul and will adjust their words accordingly" (5:25). The soul being the recipient of spiritual knowledge is the place of growing conscious awareness of God. This is the soul's subtle work to which we must attend with vigilance and prudence.

In Philip's wisdom, the soul is attached either to our mental cognition (the self-centered mind) or to the heart's knowing (God-centered consciousness). As we learn to live increasingly in communion with Spirit, our ego-intelligence and separate-self decreases, becoming diminished. Enlightenment comes as the soul gains knowledge of God. Philip says, "those who gain wisdom from Truth are liberated beings" (3:29). This knowledge of God gives us our freedom to become the innate and veritable selves we essentially are, freed from our societal and cultural conditionings. St.

---

[5] Walshe, *Sermons and Treatises, Volume 3*, Fragment of an Unknown Sermon, 131.

Symeon the New Theologian gave witness to this experience in his own life:

> As I was meditating, Master, on these things, suddenly You appeared from above, much greater than the Sun and You shone brilliantly from the heavens down into my heart. . . O what intoxication of light, O what movement of fire! O what swirlings of the flame in me, miserable one that I am, coming from You and Your glory! The glory I know it and I say it is Your Holy Spirit...but while I was there, surrounded by darkness You appeared as Light, illuminating me completely from Your total light. And I became light in the night.[6]

THE SOUL'S WORK

Regarding this new orientation of the soul towards the Holiest of Holy Places, Philip cautions,

> It is good to come out of this world's system into that place where humankind existed before it became lost.... There are those, of course, who neither long for this, nor are they capable of accomplishing it. And still others who, though they wish for it, can never achieve it because they have no sustained practice (3:15).

This work returns us to our original state, as "a little child" again, where we're open to be recreated in transcendence.

[6] Maloney, *Saint Symeon the New Theologian*, Hymn 25, 301.

This is the path of becoming whole and one, uniting the image with the archetype, the inner with the outer person, the state of resurrection.

Philip seems to indicate that there are three possible stages of existence: this world into which we've been born where choices are made; a second place of spiritual "resurrection" which connects us to our original state found in this life now; or a third condition, which after death is an intermediate state where we are "wandering about in limbo" (3:14), not finding rest or fulfillment. As an intermediate state, "limbo" implies transition and Philip adds, "only Yeshua knows what the destiny of such a person will be" (3:19). The implication is that people in limbo are still in Yeshua's care and work.

Nothing in the Gospel of Philip implies a belief in an eternal hell as it was later articulated by imperial Christianity. Philip's ultimate consolation seems to be that those who "went astray" in this life will be embraced in the next by "the Son of Humanity, the Master who has brought the children into created being" (4:24) who is "redeeming everything in the cosmos both good and evil" (5:4). Still, Philip insists that we are to find resurrected life here and now, not something for a future life.

His emphasis is on this life, where we have full volition, and where transcendence is found. The Master gave us the path of interior praxis, a remembrance of God's presence and the knowledge of ourselves that will set us free. It's a gift that, sustained over time, brings us to our highest realization and a new state of transcendence. "Anyone unreceptive to the transcendent continues on in lower realities" (3:33). This is God's work and God's creative imagination, and our part is to offer God a receptive state of being. Unless I am prepared and receptive, what Philip calls "virginal," this essential work cannot happen.

This seminal practice is what the later desert ascetics called *mneme Theo*, "remembering God," or sometimes "magnetization to God."[7] Through this soul work "one is brought into the truth of the restoration of all things" (2:8). "Remembering God," which is not simply a mental awareness, happens as we still ourselves to such an extent that we're awakened to the presence of God "in whom we live, and move, and have our being" (Acts 17:28). As Isaac the Syrian said:

> Only when we enter stillness can our souls distinguish the passions and prudently search out her own wisdom. Then our innermost self also awakens for spiritual work and day by day we perceive the hidden wisdom which blossoms forth in our souls . . . Stillness mortifies the outward senses and resurrects the inward movements, whereas the outward manner of life does the opposite, that is, it resurrects the outward senses and deadens the inward movements.[8]

Few seem to be able to take this innermost journey, as it is arduous and requires we turn from our egos. But here the author, once again, breaks through with a personal concern, "in this world one can exist either in the realm of resurrection, or in a domain between [this world and the resurrection). May it be that I am not found in the latter place! In that region, which is death, pure evil does exist" (3:14). We're given this short, but immensely privileged life to evolve and

---

[7] Robin Amis, *A Different Christianity* (State University of New York, 1995), 190.
[8] Hilarion Alfeyev, *The Spiritual World of Isaac the Syrian* (Liturgical Press, 2008), 81.

become complete, but it requires our volition and utter participation. This journey is deadly to the separate ego and is anathema to our social constructs.

Our only other choice is death, where, Philip cautions, volition is no longer possible. This is the point of the author's concern. Now is the possibility, and it is here in our present state that all things are possible. Another wonderful and unique quote of Jesus by Philip states, "the Master said: 'Some have attained the Realm of heaven laughing'" (2:21). Their laughter is their knowledge of the foolishness of clinging to this world's system, which they now see as simply a "game being played." The promise is, "These came forth from out of this world rejoicing" (2:21)—into transcendent realities, here and now.

If indeed this is an authentic quote by Jesus, laughter is, indeed, a wise response to the ludicrous seriousness with which so much of our society takes itself, with the belief that they know the truth when in fact they're blind and unable to see. "Authorities seek to control and enslave us so that we will not recognize our true reality" (5:13). Clinging to our self-defenses and ego-centrality only keeps us "slaves of our own offenses," Philip tells us (3:29).

Our spiritual evolution requires the deepest surrender and submission to God's will possible, and an ongoing cleansing of all that is not of God. "For it is 'desire' itself that turns many towards wrongdoing, and the absence of hunger for right-relatedness both blocks a deeper desire and the ability to bring it about" (3:15). When we accept this, we face that edifice of our ego's construction, built over a lifetime, and begin its deconstruction. Eckhart said,

> Whoever has gone out of themselves so far that they are the only-begotten Son would

> own all that the only-begotten Son owns. God performs all God's works that we may become the only-begotten Son. When God sees that we are the only-begotten Son, God is in such haste that God may reveal to us the plenitude of God's being and God's nature: God then hastens to make it our own just as it is God's own. Here God has delight and joy in abundance. Those who stand in God's ken and in God's love, become none other than what God is Godself."[9]

Philip puts it this way:

> That which the Father possesses belongs also to the children, but as long as they remain in their infancy, nothing is ever entrusted to them. When, however, they mature, all that the Father possesses he willingly gives to them. (3:26)

PURIFYING THE SELF

Philip intriguingly tells us that in this world one of our dilemmas is that "evil is not pure evil and good not pure good" (3:14). We are always earth-beings that are of the humus but also light-beings filled with Spirit. The fact that we are earthly means that we are never "pure" spiritual beings, but an amalgamation that uses the humus of life as a means of becoming more and more of the Light. The Gospel of Thomas tells us:

---

[9] Walshe, *Meister Eckhart Sermons and Treatises, Volume 2*, Sermon 57, 84.

> Yeshua says, Suppose you are asked, "Where have you come from?" say, "We have come from the Light at its source, from the place where it came forth and was manifest as Image and Icon." If you are asked, "Are you that Light?" say, "We are its children, and chosen by the Source, the Living Father."[10]

The tension between our inner self and our outer self will always be with us while we are earthly beings on the physical plane, and Light beings in the spiritual sphere.

Philip says we must face evil within ourselves in order to purify ourselves from our impediments to wholeness (3:23). In this esoteric prayer we will come to see that "the roots of evil are hidden within and are strong." Thus, Philip says, we must "delve deeply into our own hearts to the root of evil and bring it out...naming it for what it is." As Jesus said in the Gospel of Thomas:

> Grapes are not harvested from thorns, nor are figs gathered from thistles—neither produce fruit. Good people bring goodness out of a storehouse of inner treasure, and evil ones bring wickedness out of the repository of evil collected in the heart. It is from there that they speak. For from the heart's overflow evil enters the world.[11]

Philip quotes Jesus in concert with Matthew 3:10: "The axe has already been applied to the root of the tree" (3:22). We hear him saying that the Creator has brought us into

---

[10] The Gospel of Thomas, 50, 24.
[11] The Gospel of Thomas, 45, 22.

such a conscious state that the separation from our unconscious behavior needs to be examined and faced in order to be healed. In this practice we are freed to become the being we were created to be. The truth of who we already are. Becoming conscious of the roots of evil within ourselves is the first step toward repentance and change.

Evil is the parts of ourselves that are contrary to love and have taken root, causing harmful behavior. The second step in forgiveness is to name it, seeing its rootedness within us, bringing it into the "Perfect Light" where it withers, thus freeing us to find our unity with God and all creation restored. "Let us delve deeply into our own hearts to the root of evil and tear it out. If it is recognized for what it is, it will be uprooted...and will perish" (3:23). This is our path to freedom and restoration to fullness. Philip implies that this is a formal rite of passage. As we are coming to know ourselves at our deepest level, we will increasingly face all barriers to our transformation.

Jesus taught us to see and face those things within us that separate us from God, that is, those things that are not of love and harm ourselves and our relationships with fellow human beings. "Forgive us as we forgive others" (Matthew 6:12) is the only path to our restoration to wholeness. We cannot find our own freedom and wholeness until all our relationships are healed. This requires our total self-negation, for this is not the work of the ego, but of the heart and love. Only our essential self, recreated in God's image, can do this work with detachment from our self-interest. This is our inner observer, seeing through the eyes of God, the eyes of love, detached from self-defense. The ego-mind only judges and makes comparisons, defending itself. The heart, rather, sees in truth and clarity, with godly eyes of compassion and wisdom.

Exorcism of the evil we discover within cannot begin until we enter the second chamber of consciousness, the Holy of Holies. Our minds cannot do the work because our egos cannot repair themselves. This is the work only of those who "have gained wisdom from truth" (3:29). Love opens the eyes of our hearts. Love empowers the work and love severs the roots. Only in our transcendent detached state, in unity of being, can we discern what is of Love (God) in us and what isn't.

CHAPTER 4
THE HOLIEST OF HOLY PLACES: BRIDAL CHAMBER

> Winds of the south and winds of the north,
> wake up and blow now: breathe through my
> garden,
> drive him mad with my frangrance, draw him
> into my garden;
> let his tongue stop its talking, let it taste my
> choice fruits.
> (Song of Songs 4:15)

The third chamber, "opens to the East, which is the Holiest of the Holiest of all where only the High Priest may enter" (1:2). Philip teaches that only those prepared and virginal may enter this most sacred chamber to commune with God in this hidden place within ourselves. The East, of course, is where the sun rises, where full knowledge is gained, and the light reveals our deepest understanding. Like our first birthing into the earthly realm, this is a rebirth into the heavenly realm here and now, where we discover we're One as God is One.

Philip calls this holiest chamber an "ark of safety for us, a place of refuge when the waters of cataclysm overwhelm us" (1:5). We are temples of God, a discovery we make as we awaken to the truth of our own selves. Jesus said, "You shall know the truth and the truth will set you free," Philip says (4:1), either quoting from John's Gospel (8:32), or sharing

John's source. Free to be the mature child of God we were meant to become. Free to let the God within us be God in and through us. Free to give birth to our truest selves as we become the Christ, married beings at one with God without division. "If we unite intimately with it [Truth] we shall reach ultimate fulfillment" (4:1).

This innermost chamber of the Jerusalem Temple held the Ark of the Covenant, containing the ten commandments, and is where the presence of God, the *Shekinah*, was understood to reside. This was the holiest of holy places and inaccessible to anyone but the high priest of the temple. Likewise, this holiest of holy places is a sanctuary for us, a presence within us full of silence, peace, and love. As we make this transcendent journey, we are shown a perspective of our world only seen from the inside out. Here we know that through our earthly struggles something immense is waiting to be born. And here Philip uses a further metaphor to describe our relationship with God. Something beyond us is awakening within, as we become "mothers of God." This knowledge, rather than something gained, is a discovery of who we already are, "Beings of Light," at One with "Perfect Light."

Having become virginal, we are brought into the marriage chamber to unite with and marry the Beloved, and consequently give birth to the Christ, "the True Light which illumines all humankind" (John 1:8). This new human is the highest pinnacle for the human race, as we evolve into our fullness of being.

> This new race bears the name "True human"
> in this world, and it is here, in this very place,
> where they become the sons and daughters of
> the Bridal Chamber. (4:11)

We should note that this "progression" through the chambers of the temple is contrary to nature and its usual progression (1:2). Rather than beginning in the east with the rising of the sun and ending in the west, we begin in the west, at the ingathering of our lives, having been prepared for this primary journey of our souls through spiritual maturation. Having already formed the outer person, we now turn to our soul's development. This work is entirely of the Spirit. This passage is only possible for the mature or initiated.

It would at first appear that this journey through the inner chambers of our being is sequential and charted by time, but it's not. This spiritual and esoteric journey into greater consciousness is outside of our timeframes and patterns. For Jesus, Philip says, this progression through the inner chambers took place at his baptism and in fullness (5:1). For each of us, this journey is guided and taught us by the Spirit of God as we are prepared and made ready. It is more like a dance and a song, not linear but orchestrated and flowing in spiritual patterns of evolution and transformation. Often this is experienced as outside of our own mental cognition but known by the heart and revealed in new sentience and deportment. Discernment, according to Philip, in this regard is the domain of our hearts (4:1). Our hearts open us to perception beyond that of our minds and is evidenced by the enlargement of our capacity for love.

THE ART OF LIVING

Who is this blessed one,
blooming like the dawn,
radiant as the moon,
pure as the fire of the sun,

> as awesome and fearsome
> as the procession of the stars
> through the sky of night? (Song of Songs 6:10)

"Ignorance grounded in confusion is the mother of evil," states Philip. And Jesus says in Thomas, humans "are blind. They cannot see from within."[1] So ignorance is the human condition and it is where we all begin. Left in this condition, according to Philip, we will turn against our creator and against creation itself. But Philip is optimistic, because ignorant people can have the eyes of their hearts opened. It is possible to see from within. It's our creator's plan and the whole purpose of our earthly sojourn: "Truth...triumphs over ignorance and liberates us from confusion" (4:1). The direct path to this knowledge is communion with God.

By this, we are enlightened, and we discover the immensity of the art of living. God becomes present to us, and to equate this communion with marriage is to give a clearer picture of the new relationship. The prophet Isaiah spoke of it as a mystical experience:

> For as a young man marries a young woman, so shall your builder marry you, and as the bridegroom rejoices over the bride, so shall your God rejoice over you. (Isaiah 62:5)

This experience of God isn't intellectual, or a set of beliefs, but rather a loving relationship where each entity (God and I) accedes their individual distinctiveness and become one through a deep penetration into the other. In this spiritual marriage, we unite each other's unfathomable

[1] The Gospel of Thomas, 28, 18.

depths, we become accessible to the other, offering ourselves in a new unity of being. I lose my separate "self," but I, in turn, become a new reality, an unprecedented manifestation of God in new fullness [*pleroma*], true to my unique essential self. "In this way," the Anointed One, "completes the right relationship with all things" (2:22).

The Song of Songs sings of this union:

> I will drink the finest of wines
> from your lips, wine that flows gently
> from your mouth to mine, as we
> lie together, out of time. (7:10)

To the uninitiated, it might all appear strangely abstruse and reserved for an elite few. But it is an experience meant for everyone.

Since human sexuality is the icon that leads us to this secret bridal chamber, it shows us how intrinsic it indeed is. Most of us have had glimpses of this spiritual marriage when, having lost ourselves in creativity, sexual love, compassion, or in deep expressions of our true selves, have experienced something transcendent. God is always waiting, present to unite with us, thus giving birth to greater truth, beauty, and goodness through our self-emptiness and newfound creativity. When we are full of ourselves, we are absent to God, but when we are empty of ourselves, we are open to God, and God is veritable there. Isaac the Syrian speaks to this experience:

> Strive to enter your inner chamber, and you will behold the heavenly chamber, for this and that are one, and by one entrance you will see both. The ladder of that kingdom is within you,

> hidden in your soul. Plunge in and cleans yourself from sin, and you will find there the rungs by which you can ascend.[2]

This progression through the inner chambers is not a natural process, but a supernatural or metaphysical work, outside space and time. "These have been received into the Realm of the Blessed where the Logos has uplifted their souls," Philip explains (5:5). This is the domain of the heart alone. He goes on to say, "Those begotten in God's heart are called and nourished there in order that they might reach the promised destiny of transcendence." And "Anyone who is born a child from the Bridal Chamber...has been vested with light, and the powers that be can neither see nor seize them" (4:15). They are hidden from the world, but the world has already become for them the "Great Age of the Eternal Now" (4:15).

HOLY DESIRE

> Oh daughters of Jerusalem, swear to me here—
> that our desire not be disturbed
> till our fire we have quenched.
> (Song of Songs 8:4)

The evangelist Matthew tells us that at Jesus' death, as he gave up his spirit "suddenly, the curtain in front of the Holy of Holies was ripped in half from top to bottom" (Matthew 27:51). This curtain, according to Philip, "was torn in two to reveal the Bridal Chamber, which is nothing other than the image of the heavenly Temple" (1:4). It tells us this happened

[2] Isaac the Syrian, *Ascetical Homilies: The Full Collection* (Virgin Mary of Australia and Oceania, 2024), Homily 30, 102.

"so that all might have access to the truth of hidden things." And further, "This truth...strengthens us to go inward...and by this lowly means to enter into the presence of the fullness of glory...and thus saints and sacred beings bring us to the threshold of the Bridal Chamber and invite us within" (1:7). This is the crux of the matter, for Philip, and the vision of why Jesus submitted to his death on the cross. Our salvation is based on this truth that he manifested to the whole world. God's reign comes not by way of physical power and human will but by taking the hidden, secret path to the inner core of our own being, where entering the heavenly realm we marry God.

This is our invitation to discover the divine goodness of the many things. "When the Anointed One came he brought interiority into the external world" (3:13)—where we find God present at the ground of all being. Only through this innermost sight can we see and know through "spiritual love." Jesus promised in the Gospel of Thomas, "I disclose my mysteries to those ready for Mystery."[3] And Philip speaks to this deepest of human mysteries: "There is magnificence to the mystery of marital union...so, contemplate, then, the union of pure spiritual embrace, for it has great power. Its image (marriage) is found in physical sexual union" (4:4).

This contemplation of the pure spiritual embrace is not cognition. It is not thinking about this experience, but rather con-templing the event. Entering the temple of my own being, the "marriage chamber" where I receive the knowledge of marital union gained only in the experience of this "pure spiritual embrace." Like physical sexual union, which gives us deep knowledge of our loves and spouses, we can only know God through the experience of loving

[3] The Gospel of Thomas, 62, 28.

God, where there is a breakthrough of each into the other bringing about a oneness of being. This is the direct route to knowledge of God.

> I am yours, beloved, and you are my desire.
> Come. Let's go out, into the country.
> We can spend the night in the little villages there.
> There I will give you what you have waited for.
> The scent of the mandrakes is breathing in the door.
> Come out; at the doorstep there awaits every pleasure
> that I have kept locked away for my lover. (Song of Songs 7:11-12,14)

Although this is a metaphor for our union with God that is ancient—in both Jewish and Christian traditions—for Western Christians it might still come as a shock. The emphasis in the West has long been upon the pure state of physical virginity as a spiritually superior state. The Roman Catholic Church still requires celibacy for clergy, a result of long years of the Church keeping a general tone toward sex and marriage largely as a concession to human weakness, for those unable to embrace celibacy or a celibate marriage. The Church father, Origen (186-254 CE), who castrated himself to overcome his sexual proclivities, brought suspicion on sexuality by teaching that Eve was seduced sexually by the serpent, and so concluded that sex, even within marriage, was inherently wrong. Later, Augustine (354-430) taught that marriage was ordained of God for propagation purposes only and said if couples could refrain from sex while married, that was a better state. These ideas prevailed in the Church and many theologians even disdained the sexual act as a degradation of the flesh. Philip, by contrast says, "Sacred beings are entirely holy, including their bodies. And everything they touch is also purified" (3:2). The imperial Church came shockingly close to Gnosticism when it disparaged the physical body and its sensuality. It was blind to this remarkable and more ancient Christian teaching on sacred marriage.

For Philip, sexuality is not just holy but the highest expression of the "mysteries." Not only is sex good and righteous, but the icon revealing how we come to a knowledge of God through participation in God. Marriage is generative, bringing new life into the world, and even more so is the "union of pure spiritual embrace" (4:4). Sexuality teaches and prepares us for sacred marriage with the knowledge of how all things are restored to wholeness through their unity with God. For this reason, Philip encourages us to contemplate the mystery of marital union. It reveals our path to the healing of the earth. "The Anointed One comes to receive back what he has always loved...redeeming everything in the cosmos, both good and evil" (5:4).

CONSIDER JESUS AND MARY MAGDALENE

Philip speaks of Jesus' relationship to the Apostle Miriam of Magdala, "for the Master appeared to love her more than the other students, and many times would kiss her on the mouth" (4:9).[4] The Gospel of Mary Magdalene speaks of this relationship as well. In it, Peter is quoted saying to Mary, "Sister, we know that the Savior greatly loved you

[4] A damage to the codex takes place here and the place of the kiss is missing! The answer puzzles all translators, but most scholars believe the answer is "on the mouth" or lips, as that is most consistent with Jewish mysticism, and any other body part would not make sense considering Jewish culture.

above all other women, so tell us what you remember of his words that we ourselves do not know or perhaps have never heard."[5] Jesus was fully human, "Son of Humanity," according to Philip, and also "Master" of the spiritual life. Mary Magdalene being one of Jesus' disciples, had a special and unique relationship with him by all accounts. Philip points out that "there were three named 'Miriam' who continuously walked with the Master: his mother, his sister and Magdalene who was called his companion. Thus, Miriam is his mother, his sister, and his mate" (4:8).

Jesus, Philip argues, had a human father,[6] for why would he speak of "my father in heaven" if he didn't have an earthly father (4:7)? Philip also says, "On that cross [Joseph's] own seed hung" (5:20). His mother Mary, according to Philip, conceived as every human mother does—through sex with a man. "Jesus of Nazareth was begot of Mary and Joseph" (John 1:45). The miracle of Jesus' birth wasn't its extraordinary and unhuman experience, but rather its ordinariness. That God was in the birth as active agent is the teaching. God's involvement in human sexual activity is the insight, and opens and challenges our perspective of sexuality completely.

In Philip's understanding the fact that Jesus was begot of Mary and Joseph was sacred and good, and led to the birth of a human child who was to become a fully realized human being, the "Son of Humanity," Jesus the Anointed One. It would not be surprising, then, for Philip to see Jesus

---

[5] The Dialogues of Mary Magdalene, Dialogue 2, 67.

[6] In Philip 5:21 it says, "Adam came into being from two virgins: the Spirit and the virgin earth. The Anointed One, therefore, was also born of a virgin so that the stumbling which occurred at the beginning, might be rectified." This passage appears on the surface to support a "virgin birth," however, in other places virginity is used metaphorically, as it was with Meister Eckhart, referencing a state of the soul's purity.

as a sexual being, having normal sexual relations, but we will not know the answer to that question conclusively and it's unimportant here. Philip's insight is that sexuality with all its complexities is God-given, God-blessed, and God-involved. It is intended to be simply one of the holiest of human sacred behaviors.

The Greek word *koinonos* translated as companion and mate in Philip 4:8 has many meanings. It is inconclusive here. *Koinonos* could refer to a close friendship or discipleship, but it could also be referring to a marriage partner. We can't assume that Jesus was married to Mary Magdalene, but we are invited to see that he had an intimate and deeply spiritual relationship with her, which involved a tender kiss. We should remember, however, that in Philip the outer form or literal meaning of words is not the depth of what is meant. Philip speaks in metaphors and allegories throughout. Thus, the kiss has many meanings and we could take it on any level of understanding, but most deeply, the kiss refers to our most profound expressions of love and understanding. This is reminiscent of the Song of Songs, which begins:

> Oh, kiss me, touch me with your lips:
> your love tastes better than any wine.
> You smell better than any perfume;
> Even the sound of your name smells sweet—
> no wonder they all love you! (Song of Songs 1:1)

In Jewish mysticism, the kiss is understood to be the exchange of the breath that occurs through kissing, when "spirits join—as each one gives of his or her own spirit while partaking of the spirit of the other."[7] It's the deepest

[7] Joel Hecker, "The Kiss: From Metaphor to Mysticism," TheTorah.com (2021).

expression of love that results in the mystical union of the soul and God and the union of love between humans. Jewish mysticism gives us clues to Jesus' relationship with Mary Magdalene.

When Philip tells us that Jesus often kissed Mary Magdalene on the lips, it's speaking of a deep, spiritual connection, beyond the physical. One that speaks of a soulful knowledge of one another and the joining of spirits; a spiritual marriage. Philip goes on to say that "we should desire to kiss one another and assist in each other's conception through the love we mutually share" (4:10). And here Philip is again using metaphors. The "kiss" which we give to one another is meeting each other spirit to spirit at the deepest level of our beings. And with this love we are united in sacred marriage, for "God is Spirit" (John 4:24). "Those who abide in love abide in God, and God abides in them" (1 John 4:16). Above all, we are to understand that Jesus' relationship with Mary was sacred and spiritually transcendent, not simply of fleshly desire.

Philip is not afraid of talking about sexual love for it teaches, and reveals the path to transcendence for humanity. Physical love opens a window into the internal workings of our evolutionary forces, for they are based on the energy of love. Love is an action and must be manifested. It isn't something that's merely felt, or an emotion. "We are caused to love in order to give" Philip teaches (3:32). Spiritual love means giving of ourselves for the sake of the world, that needs unconditional love and this healing balm for its brokenness. When this new humanity is birthed into the world as "masters over all" (2:21) they will continue the work of Christ in finishing creation. Spiritual love in all its forms is medicine to heal our broken world. Love in all its variations, beginning with physical love and reaching to transcendence, is the path to wholeness. Wherever there is love, there is God. Whoever partakes in this spiritual kiss is given knowledge of God.

> My children, our love must not be simply words or mere talk—it must be true love, which shows itself in action and truth. This, then, is how we'll know we belong to the truth; this is how we'll be confident in God's presence. (1 John 3:18-19)

Spiritual Consummation

Orthodox forms of Christianity teach that believing certain theological statements is a sign of belonging, but this is erroneous and dangerous and shallow. For Philip, knowledge comes last, not first. What binds us together is our love for each other; from this will come knowledge of God.

The color of water is that of the vessel containing it, and so is the soul. To truly exemplify truth, we will know it by the color of our actions. Since we can be self-deluded, our work in self-denial, as Jesus said, is the only path to that reality. We cannot truly love until we have turned our backs on our self-centrality—we'll only see our own behavior through that lens.

"Those who were separated shall be united, and all who are empty shall be filled, so that everyone may enter into the Bridal Chamber where they will be born into the Light," Philip says (4:33). Philip understands this experience of communion as a *daily practice* where, "remembering God," we seek continual ongoing union with God (4:32). Like our human sexual behavior, we seek it again and again as our desires and longings draw us back to intimate relationship with God.

"Standing together" in spiritual love, according to Philip, is a necessary component of spiritual work (3:31).

In relationships we come into oneness of being, as we find deeper unity with one another. Companionship is of paramount importance, for it is how we nurture and assist each other through this spiritually transformative endeavor. Using another metaphor, it says Love is the "anointing" that brings enlightenment and the remedy for the human spiritual illness, which according to Philip is ignorance. Sharing this "healing oil" is the bond of companionship. Without it, Philip warns, we "stagnate." We need each other, for love is only active in relationships and possible in companionship. Since love is the medicine that heals us, we must "kiss one another," in a "pure spiritual embrace." This way, we will "assist in each other's conception" (4:10)—that is, spiritual marriage.

Love begins as we experience God's love for us, bringing light to our innermost identities. This love then reaches beyond us to others. As we join with truth in spiritual marriage we find our wholeness and our highest receptive state for "spiritual love is truly a fragrance-filled-wine meant to be enjoyed by all who receive it" (3:31). Meister Eckhart said, "Nothing brings you closer to God or makes God so much your own as the sweet bond of love."[8]

"So," Philip says, "neither fear the flesh nor love it. For if you fear it, it will become your master, and if you love it, it will devour and suffocate you" (4:20). The flesh is holy and with holy beings it has a holy and beautiful purpose. Creation is made and shaped by love. God is love, and thus love is the essential energy at the core of all being. And in spiritual marriage we find the "truth of the restoration of all things" (2:8). In the Gospel of Mary Magdalene, Jesus is quoted saying, "the Good has come among you pursuing its

[8] Walshe, *Meister Eckhart Sermons and Treatises, Volume 1,* Sermon 4, 46.

own essence within nature in order to unite everything with its origin."[9] Spiritual marriage is the destiny of all creation!

Philip tells us that we existed with God prior to our sojourn on earth, and are now returning to God, "that place where humankind existed before it became lost" (3:14). Philip quotes Jesus saying: "Blessed are all who existed before coming into being" (5:28). We are blessed when we come to understand our essential nature in God, an eternal existence. The earth sojourn is a necessary evolution, as we come to this new transcendent state of being, drawn to God by our deep longings, which is our human destiny and a new birthing of the Christ, "in order to fill the whole universe" (Ephesians 4:10).

How beautiful it is to raise human sexuality from something merely physical to its highest spiritual and holy potential! Realizing that desire itself is holy helps us to love ourselves, and know that we are not made to denigrate those basic hungers. That God entices and woos us to Godself for a spiritual embrace reveals the depths of God's love. This also reveals Philip's Jewish mystical roots as found in the prophet Hosea:

> On that day, says the Beloved One, you will call me, "My husband,"... And I will take you for my wife forever. I will take you for my wife in righteousness and in justice, in steadfast love, and in mercy. I will take you for my wife in faithfulness, and you shall know me. (Hosea 2:16, 20)

Desire and longing open us and make us hunger not just for physical love, but more profoundly for our

---

[9] The Dialogues of Mary Magdalene, 65.

deepest spiritual consummation. All desires ultimately are a yearning for God, as they are meant to lure and bring us to the Beloved One awaiting within. Love in Philip's sense is the force within all things seeking to find union with another. God is a Lover luring us to the bridal chamber at the core of our being. No wonder Philip says spiritual love is "meant to be enjoyed by all." How could the imperial Church have missed this most profoundly beautiful and deepest of spiritual mysteries?

GNOSIS: KNOWLEDGE OF GOD

Philip says, "ignorance grounded in confusion is the mother of evil" (4:1). This is the dilemma for most of us. As Jesus the Christ said in the Gospel of Thomas:

> I stood to my feet in the midst of the cosmos, appearing outwardly in flesh. I discovered that all were drunk but none were thirsty, and my soul ached for the children of humanity. For their hearts are blind. They cannot see from within. They have come into the cosmos empty, and they are leaving it empty.[10]

Ignorance—and with it, emptiness and confusion—keeps us on the outside, seeking but never seeming to find. We see how beautiful and peaceful the world can be, and yet remain discontent and confused, detached from and outside of God. Our hearts are restless.

This is the beginning of our awakening, because we see how we are caught up, confused, with potential for evil,

---

[10] The Gospel of Thomas, 28, 18.

caught on the outside, and detached from life. Going in circles, we hunger for initiation, and are ultimately guided to our own innermost chambers. There, seeing from within, we learn to stop, listen, and open our hearts to what our Master and Teacher is speaking. Again in Thomas Jesus says, "Whoever drinks what flows from my mouth will come to be as I am and I also will come to be as they are, so that what is hidden will become manifest."[11]

Philip explains: "If truth is fully revealed [we] can be brought to perfection. It is ignorance that enslaves us, and enlightenment which liberates us" (4:1). This truth is found "within our hearts. If we unite intimately with it, we shall reach ultimate fulfillment" (4:1). We will never know God through conceptual knowledge, standing apart objectifying God. We can only know God in relationship, in the bridal chamber: "I will take you for my wife and you will know me" (Hosea 2:20), says our Creator. There's no other path to enlightenment.

> Seal me around your heart, love,
> like the bracelets around your arm.
> Love is stronger than death, and as unrelenting.
> I am jealous of your love;
> my heart bursts for you like the fire of God.
> No water could ever put out this fire, love;
> no flood could wash it away.
> (Song of Songs 8:6-7)

That human ignorance is our primary malady might come as a surprise. We want to believe that we're enlightened beings, but many of us are unconscious of the

---

[11] The Gospel of Thomas, 108, 39.

spiritual world in which we live. We like to think we're fully conscious and awake but, in fact, our "hearts are blind and we cannot see from within."[12] Most of us live distracted lives, mired in lower realities. In Philip we read, "It is not possible for a person to see the higher realities of existence unless that person has become as real as they are" (3:4). This is our germinal situation and reason for our present dilemma and cause for the destruction of the earth. Our only hope for healing is to come to a knowledge of God. And for Philip it is the work to establish amphibious living. As we practice "remembering God," we are bringing the spiritual life within us ever more deeply into our physical, mundane lives. Our ongoing practice helps us to increasingly find and live from the well of Life within us. Jesus said, "Our words flow from the fullness of our heart: a good person brings good things out of a good storehouse; a bad person brings bad things out of a bad storehouse" (Matthew 12:34-35).

MADE TO LOVE

Only as we experientially "enter into the presence of the fullness of glory—glory upon glory, light upon light, power upon power," do we reach our sovereignty and God's fullness (1:7). This results from our participation in the innermost chambers within us, awakening us to the Presence of the One who intends to be One in all things. "There is being and there is non-being," Philip says, "but Reality is One and Whole, but still, it is not able to enter into anyone who only has a heart of flesh" (5:8).

This turning to the presence within opens us to our

---

[12] The Gospel of Thomas, 28, 18.

greatest and highest knowledge. “Those at its heart are freed and rescued” from ignorance (2:24). “Those who were separated shall be united, and all who are empty shall be filled so that everyone may...be born into the Light” (4:33). This birth is the result of our “Spiritual marriage which is consummated in the full light of day”—that is, with conscious love. A direct result of our inward journey to the divine lover who restores us to fullness. The result of this marriage is the birth of our true self—the Christ who is continuing to be born through a new humanity.

> Make no mistake about this...every worthwhile gift, every genuine benefit comes from above, descending from the Creator of the heavenly luminaries, who cannot change and is never in shadow. God willingly gave birth to us with a word spoken in truth, so that we may be, as it were, the first fruits of God’s creatures. (James 1:18)

Philip tells us that “through rest and repose children are begotten” in this world (4:29). When we become “real”—fully realized human beings—we will be able to “see the higher realities” and co-create with God. In contrast, when formed by the outer world, our cultures, and our own willpower (unaware of the higher realities), we’re incapable of spiritual sight. Isaac the Syrian speaks of this:

> Knowledge that is occupied with visible things and receives instruction concerning them through the senses, is called natural. But knowledge that is occupied with the noetic power that is within things and with incorporeal

> natures is called spiritual... But that knowledge which is occupied with divinity is called supra-natural, or rather, unknowing and knowledge-transcending.[13]

This supra-natural knowledge is not a knowing by way of the senses, but detached from them. It is an unknowing which paradoxically gives us full knowledge and clearer sight. Our struggles for transcendence are how our souls evolve. Eckhart speaks of this:

> [I]t may be called a nescience, an unknowing, yet there is in it more than in all knowing and understanding without it, for this unknowing lures and attracts you from all understood things, and from yourself as well. This is what Christ meant when he said, "Whoever will not deny themselves and will not leave father and mother, and is not estranged from all these, is not worthy of me" (Matthew 10:37), as though to say, whoever does not abandon creaturely externals can be neither conceived nor born in this divine birth. But divesting yourself of yourself and of everything external does truly give it to you. And in very truth I believe...that whoever is established in this cannot in any way ever be separated from God.[14]

Philip says, "a slave longs for freedom" (5:15). This longing is our loadstar drawing us to God. Longing is the Spirit

---

[13] Hilarion Alfeyev, *The Spiritual World of Isaac the Syrian* (Liturgical Press, 2008), 263.
[14] Walshe, *Meister Eckhart Sermons and Treatises, Volume 1*, Sermon 1, 11.

within us, our essential being and our primary evolutionary tool. Yearning for transcendence is innate to all creatures and can shape and direct our lives if Spirit directed. This requires we know and understand ourselves and are oriented toward God's presence through love. Here is when we begin to see what in us has been formed and created by our cultures and entities of lower consciousness, and what is of Spirit.

"There are times when grief does come to the virtuous, not because [Jesus] oppresses them, but because their own flaws and calamities have overwhelmed them" (5:3). There are other times when "some must endure terrible grief" as it is just the human experience (5:3). In all our pain and anguish, when seen in the light of the Spirit, we recognize that God is with us and will bring about our fullness. As the prophet Isaiah says, "My soul yearns for You in the night, and my spirit within me earnestly seeks You" (Isaiah 26:9).

Though at first this longing comes from a desire for my own wholeness, it doesn't end with myself. When awakened to the presence of God within, there will ultimately come, as a result of my spiritual marriage, a shift from a focus upon me to that of my desire for God and the greater concerns for the whole earth.

> Come, take me; carry me off
> like some wild desert chieftain to his tent;
> take me! (Song of Songs 1:4)

Until we are freed from the constrictions of the fear-based mind, we will be controlled by unconscious assumptions of our relationship to the earth, to one another, and to God. Until we understand our hunger to be met in the spiritual dominion, we will seek its answer mistakenly in the physical and mental domain. This misplaced hunger is what is driving the destruction of our society and of the earth. Philip calls us to be unmoored from our mental constrictions and be free from anthropomorphic centrality to see a new theocentric and earth-centric view marked by higher spiritual values. In The Dialogues of Mary Magdalene, she spoke so beautifully of this state of being:

> And my soul sang: "What bound me has been slain. What encompassed me has been vanquished. Desire has reached its end and I am freed from ignorance. I left one world behind with the aid of another, and now as Image I have been freed from the analog. I am liberated from the chains of forgetfulness which have existed in time. From this moment onward, I go forward into the season of the Great Age, the Aeon, and there, where time rests in stillness in the Eternity of time, I will repose in silence." And having said this Mary fell silent since it was to this point that the Savior had brought her.[15]

"We are caused to love in order that we might give. For if one gives without love, there is no benefit in the giving," says Philip (3:32). Transcendent knowledge causes a metamorphosis in our behavior. Philip goes on to tell us that "the children born from the Bridal Chamber are created to serve the sons and daughters of natural birth" (4:30). These "freeborn," as Philip calls them, now do the work of Christ "setting the captives free." Freed from their enslavement to fear; fear of self-diminishment, fear of suffering, and fear of death.

---

[15] The Dialogues of Mary Magdalene, Dialogue 3, 68-69.

However, suffering and death are a part of this earthly journey, and none of us avoids it. In fact, those who truly learn to trust in love also learn to consciously accept suffering in life. When Jesus taught us to pray, "May Your will be done on earth as it is in heaven" (Matthew 6:10), he was teaching us to accept our sojourn on earth as the will of God and purposeful. It is a necessary part of the soul's formation, if we can learn to accept it as the divine plan. Even Jesus learned obedience to God's will through his suffering, according to the Letter to the Hebrews (5:8).

Also, our "hungering and thirsting for righteousness" (Matthew 5:6) is a suffering that is endemic to our spiritual welfare and Jesus promised will be filled. We long, therefore we suffer. Through that tension we are drawn into greater unity with our divine lover who is wooing us in order that we might find our wholeness and rest.

SPIRITUAL GUIDES

Philip speaks of "saints and sacred beings" who have traversed the journey through their own experience, becoming spiritual guides for others (1:7). Since all have access to the holiest of holy places, it is imperative that those desiring it be prepared and are made "virgin," in order to enter. Only the "perfected" ones, who have experienced this passage, can guide and mentor us through this esoteric pilgrimage. Emptying ourselves of all old identities and concepts that we've clung to until now takes wise assistance from masters of the spiritual life.

Those who are mature in traversing the inner realms will always assist their students in becoming the Christ, the "freeborn," who, having gained their sovereignty will ultimately be independent of their teachers. And so just as a spiritual guide is important, so too is that guide eventually to be released. The age of the guru with absolute authority is over. Jesus dispensed this with his departure and the advent of our inner teacher and advocate. He told his students:

> I will ask the One who sent me to give you another Paraclete, another Helper to be with you always—the Spirit of truth, whom the world cannot accept since the world neither sees her nor recognizes her; but you can recognize the Spirit because she remains with you and will be within you. (John 14:16-17)

Discernment, based on our own internal authority, happens in spiritual maturity, enabling us to perceive true teachings from false. "When we come to recognize the truth, we will discover the fruits within our hearts" (4:1). We discern the teachings based on the validity of the experience itself, which should always lead to unity of being and greater freedom. When maturity is gained, our sovereignty is given, we've become fully realized humans, we will find God present in all things, and our spiritual work will be to heal the rift that occurred when humans turned against nature and began to destroy that garden of paradise in which we live.

HUMANS IN THE NATURAL WORLD

Philip says:

> When humans separate from nature, then everything begins to devour and destroy itself because there is no mutual nourishment. But

> when human beings cherish and cultivate the earth, then all things are properly fed. (5:30)

We are deluded in thinking we are separate from nature because we humans are nature. We are a part of the animal kingdom and related to the many things, and they to us. We are relations.

When we separate ourselves from the natural world, we separate ourselves from the "tree of knowledge" in the midst of the Garden, and we remain ignorant of the transcendent realm. Objectifying nature by analyzing her from the distance of the mind only leads us to a false knowledge of her.

We can only know the many things with surety in the same way we come to know God, in kinship through communion as we attain unity of being. To be restored we must remember the basic primase upon which the earth was created: "Everything arises through some form of incarnation, for everything is held there in its very heart" (2:26). "One alone is truth and yet she makes the many, and by means of many things she lovingly teaches this one truth alone to all" (2:3).

Contemplation or communion is our path to union with all creation. Only spirit to spirit do we come to a knowledge of all things and know the secrets of our universe. We cannot truly know creation from the outside but must penetrate to the core and essential nature of all things by stillness and loving attention, raising our perception above that of our mental observations to our heart's perception. In this self-forgetfulness and self-merging with spirit we come to know as God knows.

Reuniting to Spirit allows us to understand and love the many things because seeing God's countenance manifested through all things gives us their intrinsic knowledge and reorients our relationship to nature. "Once this birth has really occurred, no creatures can hinder you; instead, they will all direct you to God and this birth," says Meister Eckhart.[16]

The world no longer seems strange and foreign, but connected and spiritually potent, for we see as God sees, from the inside. The natural world draws us to itself even as we've been drawn to our own depths. God is increasingly present and we are awakening to God's image more and more and everywhere.

Jesus speaking as the Logos[17] said:

> I am the light shining upon all things. I am the sum of everything, for everything has come forth from me, and towards me everything unfolds. Split a piece of wood, and there I am. Pick up a stone and you will find me there.[18]

Oh, that we had such sight! Transcendent Love is what will restore our relationship with all creation, intuiting the necessity of setting the many things free to fulfill their own essential being. The many things, like humanity, find wholeness similarly in sacred marriage, which gives them their original purpose, and eternal reality, "seeing" as God sees.

---

[16] Walshe, *Meister Eckhart Sermons and Treatises, Volume 1*, Sermon 4, 45.

[17] "The Word [Logos] was coming into the world—was in the world—and though the world was made through the Word, the world didn't recognize it. Though the Word came to its own realm, the Word's own people didn't accept it. Yet any who did accept the Word, who believed in that Name, were empowered to become children of God—children born not of natural descent, nor urge of flesh nor human will—but born of God. And the Word became flesh and stayed for a little while among us; we saw the Word's glory—the favor and position a parent gives an only child—filled with grace, filled with truth" (John 1:9-14).

[18] The Gospel of Thomas *77*, 32

Meister Eckhart reflects on this: "All creatures tend towards their ultimate perfection.... All creatures give up their life in favor of being. All creatures enter my understanding that they may become [understood] in me. I alone prepare all creatures for their return to God. Take care, all of you, what you do!"[19] In us, now, the many things find unity of being as our spirit communes with the Spirit in all things.

In God's realm, we are each a mind within the greater mind, and a consciousness within the cosmic consciousness, and all is a microcosm of the great macrocosmic universe, reflecting the whole in a multiplicity of disparate parts. God is the ground of being of all. "There is being and there is non-being, but Reality is One and Whole," says the Gospel of Philip (5:8). The Gospel of Mary Magdalene also quotes Jesus speaking in like terms:

> All of nature with its forms and creatures exist together and are interwoven with each other. They will be resolved back, however, to their own proper origin, for the compositions of matter return to the original roots of their nature. Those who have ears, let them hear this.[20]

[19] Walshe, *Meister Eckhart Sermons and Treatises, Volume 2,* Sermon 56, 80.
[20] The Dialogues of Mary Magdalene, Dialogue 1, 65.

CHAPTER 5

THE GREAT RESTORATION: CULTIVATING THE WORLD

Where we humans go in our evolutionary trajectory, all creation follows in our wake. "When human beings cherish and cultivate the earth, then all things are properly fed," Philip explains (5:30). When the ego leads with greed and self-focused living, we impede nature, of which we are relations. But when we become beings of love, and begin the outpouring of Godself "sowing the seeds of trust, hope, love, and enlightenment," then all creation will be nurtured and brought into union (5:32).

Humanity is presently sowing the seeds of doubt, despair, hate, and ignorance, and we are seeing the disastrous consequences. But it can change. As we become transformed, a new humanity can emerge bringing forth the realm of God. Jesus said, "See, I have sown fire into the cosmos, and I shall guard it carefully until it blazes."[1]

The cardinal direction of north is not mentioned in these chambers of consciousness, but it is implied. North is the place of mystery, characterized by winter, waiting, and the Divine *kenosis*. It also points to the Sabbath and the ultimate fullness of creation. North holds the other seasons in tension, in anticipation and gestation. The earth is in winter, in Philip's metaphor, for it lies dormant, awaiting the

[1] The Gospel of Thomas, 10, 11.

Spirit's enlivening. This tarrying cannot be thwarted nor hurried. There must be ongoing cultivation and preparation as we usher the earth into its fullness. "The harvest is abundant. The reapers are few. Implore the Master of harvest to send out workers," Jesus said.[2]

"Winter," according to Philip, "symbolizes the world" itself, the cosmos (5:31). Winter holds the earth in anticipation until it is ready for spring and the fullness to come. This is the *great preparation*.[3] As we take the journey into the inner chambers of our being, we're transformed into greater wholeness for the sake of the many things. Our essential self then emerges giving birth to the Christ, to assist all things in finding unity. This work, though seeming to be for the benefit of the few, is an engagement with the universal community. In this sense, winter is a Sabbath and a completion as we find rest from our greatest endeavor, becoming fully realized human beings, which is the Christ completing his mission.

"In Christ the fullness of divinity lives in bodily form, and in Christ you find your own fulfillment," reads Colossians 2:9-10. We are not whole until we are married with the Divine and bound by love. This is why Jesus prayed:

> As you have sent me into the world, so I have sent them into the world; I consecrate myself now for their sakes, that they may be made holy in truth. I don't pray for them alone. I pray also for those who will believe in me through their message, that all may be one, as you Abba, are in me and I in you; I pray that they may be one in

---

[2] The Gospel of Thomas, 73, 32.

[3] "A herald's voice cries in the desert: Prepare the way of our God, make straight the paths of God!" (Matthew 3:3)

> us, so that the world may believe that you sent me. I have given them the glory you gave me that they may be one, as we are one—I in them, you in me—that they may be made perfect in unity. (John 17:18-23)

When we have come to our fullness as human beings we can attend to the earth's wounds. The split between spirit and matter can only be healed by a marriage of the disparate realms as they are brought into balance within us. Paul speaks of this in his letter to the Ephesians: "God has taken pleasure in revealing the mystery of the plan through Christ, to be carried out in the fullness of time; namely, to bring all things—in heaven and on earth—together in Christ" (Ephesians 1:9-10).

Winter, Philip says, is a time of planting seeds and preparing the cosmos for a spring to come. "For wherever the winds of the world blow it is always winter, but when the sacred Spirit breathes it turns to summer" (2:20).

"God created the garden of paradise and humankind dwelt there, but God's desires were not in their hearts" (5:18). Being spiritually dormant we cannot see the paradise into which God has placed us. Our "hearts are blind, and we cannot see from within."[4] We are imperceptive of the iconic function of all things. We have become greedy and selfish, are detached from our own ground of being, and are devouring the earth. "When humans separate from nature, then everything begins to devour and destroy itself, because there is no mutual nourishment" (5:30). Humans are starving for the "food of paradise" and the earth is starving for spiritual nourishment!

---

[4] The Gospel of Thomas, 28, 18.

We can't see the depths of the earth's sacredness because we cannot see our own. Still, it is here that we encounter God and come to value the paradise into which we've been placed. Philip says that the "tree of knowledge in the midst of the garden" will "also enliven humanity" (5:18).

> Yeshua has come to us from the Realm of Truth and has brought us true food, and to those desiring it he gave them back their lives again so that they may never die. (5:9)

God has always been nurturing and caring for creation in ways often unknown and unseen. Endemic within the many things, the Spirit has been drawing all creation to its wholeness, "for everything arises through some form of incarnation" (2:26). From the very beginning of the cosmos God has longed to receive back what was lost when we separated from the presence of God (5:4). Our return to oneness is now the primary goal of all creation.

As Philip sees it, "our longings were elsewhere" (5:18). We were unable to "see from within," blinded by the "outer appearances."[5] Unbeknown to us the Spirit has loved and sought us, and yet humanity remained blinded to God's presence and intentions. Philip tells us that the Spirit has been energizing everything in secret, unknown to even those who took credit for her work (5:10). When we are "poor in spirit" (Matthew 5:3), God can act in and through us. In other words, the work of God takes place within the world in obscurity, beyond normal human awareness. We experience this especially in our deepest longings.

---

[5] The Gospel of Thomas, 28, 18.

UTTER HUMILITY

Though most of us are unaware because we are unconscious of her work, the Spirit is helping to evolve all peoples, cultures, and communities, working within our depths with promptings and desires. Often experiences of advancement, insight, creativity, the results of human research, inspiration, or human imagination, are in reality the Spirit within us, doing her work surreptitiously. All world religions are Spirit-inspired, if we could see it. In ignorance we can block our own creative energies which are the Spirit working in and through us. Still, God is endeavoring to hasten the earth's fulfillment through our cooperation, waiting upon our welcomed assent.

God cannot finish the creation except through human agency. The prophet Jeremiah speaks to this wholeness:

> The days are surely coming says the Lord when I will make a new Covenant.... This is the Covenant I will make with the house of Israel in those days, says the Lord: I will put my law within them, and will write it on their hearts; and I will be their God, and they shall be my people. No longer shall they teach one another, or say to each other, 'Know the Lord,' for they shall all know me, from the least of them to the greatest, says the Lord; for I will forgive their iniquity, and remember their sin no more. (Jeremiah 31:31-34)

Imperial Christianity imagines that God is an omniscient and omnipotent king with complete control, but in Philip God is portrayed as most deferential and like a lover, never coercive, never demanding, but longing, wooing, and waiting for us to enter an intimate relationship. Until then God waits humbly and silently, yet through our longing is drawing us to Godself with love. What we have misunderstood and was implicit from the beginning of creation, was God's utter self-abasement, self-giving, and subservience, making space for creation's autonomy. God is love and "love is patient.... [T]here is no limit to love's forbearance, to its trust, its hope, its power to endure" (1 Corinthians 13:4, 7). Love is only truly expressed in perfect freedom. Our creator never coerces, and the choice is always ours. Love bids us come, but it lands on us to respond.

The Genesis story tells us that "on the seventh day God had finished all the work of creation, and so on that seventh day, God rested" (Genesis 2:2). In this rest God withdrew God's power over creation, making space for our agency. In our freedom we too can find our rest from labors, which returns us to our rest in God. "For children born from the Bridal Chamber bear the same name—Rest...receiving all the glory of those who have reached fulfillment" (4:30). Rest is the condition necessary to complete creation; it is also the ontological condition of married beings. Following Jesus into the innermost chamber, the holiest of holy places, we find our rest in God; letting go of our control and domination, detaching from the separate self, in rest we marry our divine lover. "Personal accomplishment is done through effort or power, and yet through rest or repose children are begotten" (4:29).

This knowledge opens us to the greatest insights into Jesus' own death upon the cross. His crucifixion reveals his own day of rest—the ultimate self-surrender possible, "for he came to bring the system of this world to death by means of the cross," Philip explains (3:3). Philip also tells us that "all were to come under the wings of the cross" (1:5), and will thus "bear the name—Rest" (4:29). We now understand more fully Jesus' requirement for discipleship: "let them deny themselves and take up their cross" (Matthew 16:24). Self-emptiness as seen from the divine perspective in creation, and in Jesus' own life, is a necessary pattern for human fulfillment and transcendence. Only from this insight is the human experience of suffering not cataclysmic and overwhelming, but a refuge and an embrace of love (1:5). As we accept the way of the cross, resting in God's embrace, we undertake the path to human transcendence.

This knowledge challenges our old concepts of God and turns our anthropology on its head. Rather than God holding power over us, under which we must surrender or be punished, according to Philip, God is always present, lovingly seeking ways to restore our relationship (5:4). Jesus, Philip says, died to reveal to the world the folly of human egocentricity by revealing God's humility and love. Jesus' death destroyed our *modus operandi* on the cross (3:3). Rather than external power and control being how God's reign will come, it is rather through simple love, as seen in God's rest and self-giving. As Isaac the Syrian says, "the entire purpose of our Lord's death was...solely in order that the world might become aware of the love which God has for creation."[6] Divine power is being held in check, anticipating our consent and participation. This is why the world's systems, based on force and human self-aggrandizement, are doomed to fail unless, following the divine pattern, the higher path of utter humility, surrender and love is taken. We will unleash God's power from within ourselves as we give birth to the Christ in our own time and place.

---

[6] Brock, *The Wisdom of Saint Isaac the Syrian*, 27.

JOURNEY TO TRANSCENDENCE

Our journey to the transcendent realities always begins in lower intellect and unconsciousness. But this is also where grace begins and the journey to God is begun. From the human perspective we begin at our weakest, but from the transcendent perspective this is divine perfection. The Spirit always meets us where we are, and our first awakening comes through humility and detachment from self, as we learn to meet God in whom we dwell.

Then we begin to become conscious of consciousness itself, and of that which is conscious. What we deemed as inanimate becomes animate and often what we thought was animate proves inanimate. When this discovery is made the journey has begun. Ultimately this journey into God requires the rejection of all divine images and mental constructs creating a virgin soul, empty of all that is not of God. “If you do not fast from the cosmos, you will never grasp Reality,” Jesus says in the Gospel of Thomas.[7] This state of virginity opens the heart to the inflow of Spirit and our return to our Source and Creator. A breakthrough into God takes place, simultaneous with God’s breakthrough into our souls.

The Gospel of Philip describes this most clearly for us in its description of Jesus’s baptism. It offers two descriptions of the event. The first is historical and external, while the second is transcendent and internal. From an external viewpoint, Philip says:

> At the river Jordan Yeshua revealed the great fullness that is the Kingdom of the Heavens, which existed before all things. There he was

[7] The Gospel of Thomas, 27, 18.

> begotten as the Son. There he was anointed. There he was restored to fullness of being. And from there he began the great restoration. (5:1)

But then Philip wants us to understand that the meaning of this event is found, not in a belief about Jesus, but in Jesus' transcendent experience. He helps us to see that taken on the physical, historical level, this is a myth with deep meaning for humankind. But broken open we find our deepest truths. Philip is assuming that we as initiates can comprehend transcendent knowledge beyond mental cognition. "So, let us speak then of this great mystery in this way," inviting us to open the ears of our hearts:

> The Father of All came down and united with the virgin and on that day made light shine forth from the fire—revealing to us the power of the Bridal Chamber. Because of this, also on that day Yeshua came into fullness of being, coming forth from the Bridal Chamber as a bridegroom with his bride. It was also in this way that the balance of All was established in Yeshua's heart so that by means of this each of his student's might have access to enter into his rest. (5:2)

Philip is inviting us into transcendent reality, but trusting that we are able to hear, beyond the words, with the ears of our hearts the deeper meanings of this poetic, mystical, and metaphorical language. This cannot be understood at its deepest level with the mind, nor expressed rationally with words. Only our hearts are capable of this wisdom.

When Philip tells us "[On that day] the Father of All...

made light shine forth from the fire"—it is attempting to give language to a metaphysical experience. God is fire (divine energy), and in uniting with the human soul, brings new consciousness (light) into the world. We can only "know" God (or Truth) as we are "transcending" to higher intelligence, that is, permeated by the divine energy. Religions are prone to do the opposite, attempting to bring God to our cognitive level of comprehension. And in this dangerous descent we typically fall into idolatry with beliefs, dogmas, and language. This is not the level where God is known. "It is ignorance that enslaves us, and enlightenment which liberates us" (4:1).

Spiritual intelligence is the gift of our inner teacher. This knowledge we are seeking is opened to us when we are in communion with the Spirit in all things. But this "knowledge," according to Philip, is found when the outer form and the inner truth are united in a fullness of being. "Come bind our angels to our icons," Philip uniquely quotes Jesus as praying (3:10). Philip also references a quote from the Gospel of Thomas[8]: "The Master said, 'I have come to make the inner as the outer, and the outer as the inner.' Everything he said he spoke by means of signs and images concerning that place which is transcendent to this one" (2:9). May our outer persona be consonant with our inner spiritual reality. May our archetype be who we are in fullness of being. Jesus said to his disciple Salome, "I say this to you, if you become whole you will be full of Light. If you remain fragmented darkness will fill you."[9]

For Philip, God is one in all things. And as our capacities are increased, and we become "Great," for us too there will be no "other," but only unity of being (3:9). Jesus said,

---

[8] The Gospel of Thomas, 22, 17.

[9] The Gospel of Thomas, 61, 27.

"When you are able to transform two into one, then you will become a 'Son of Humanity,' and it will be possible for you to say to a mountain, 'move,' and it will move."[10] Becoming whole and unified we bring the material and spiritual planes into balance and wholeness. Then we will have returned to the garden of paradise and will nurture and care for it as intended. "The transcendence of human beings is not obvious to the naked eye. It remains hidden from view, but the result is that humans have mastery over creation" (5:29). The New Testament speaks to this:

> Divine power has given us everything we need for life and godliness through our knowledge of God, who called us to share in the divine glory and goodness. In bestowing these gifts, God has given us the guarantee of something very great and wonderful to come. Through them you'll be able to share the divine nature, and escape corruption from a world sunk in vice. (2 Peter 1:3-4)

There is no objective and absolute universal truth for all times, according to Philip. Truth is exemplified in our present encounter as we grapple with circumstances and questions, finding ways to live and address our present dilemmas and challenges. Contemplative prayer becomes our practical tool to discover what is true for us now. Truth is always ever arising as we seek her out through unity of being. Understanding is given to the degree we are united with Truth, that is with God (3:29).

---

[10] The Gospel of Thomas, 106, 39.

PARTICIPATION IN GOD

Calling God "Abba Father," was used by Jesus to awaken humanity to an entirely new understanding of God. It speaks to our lower intelligence and reveals our endemic relationship with our creator. We are not detached beings, but relations. "Father" was not a name by which God was to be called or understood, but rather a dynamic relationship to be experienced. Rather than being portrayed as some king, warrior, patriarch, or judge in a far realm, which our scriptural names imply, this relationship with "Daddy" [literally what Abba means in Aramaic] shocks us into a possible new understanding. We have spiritual DNA!

Next, Philip switches the gender, in relationship to God, according to our experience. Using the appellation "Truth" to describe the divine, Philip says, "Truth is our Mother and knowledge of her comes through joining with her" (3:29). The "mother" nature of God is seen at the core of the many things, in their ground of being. This Spirit is our Mother, for she gives birth to us in a new expression of our essential and true self. This is also where we enter the bridal chamber to commune with our divine lover, becoming one and whole. And, like Jesus, we have not "come into fullness of being" until we too have come forth from the bridal chamber in a new birthing of the Christ. Paradoxically, in this we too have become "mothers of God," birthing the Christ. So, we are not only giving birth to the Christ, in a new manifestation, but that manifestation is also our true essential self, becoming the Christ in the world in which we live.

However, none of these names or descriptions are to be taken literally. God forbid! For Philip, these are metaphors and are iconic and meant to be pedagogical pointing us to the experience of truth, in all her varied expressions and experiences. Ultimately God transcends all language, as Meister Eckhart tells us:

> God is nothing: not in the sense of having no being. God is neither *this* nor *that* that one can speak of: God is being above all being. God is beingless being. Therefore the mode of loving God must be modeless. God is beyond all speech. That we may come to this perfect love, may God help us.[11]

May God help us to come to this *nothingness* that is God. We want God to be *something* and therefore grasp at idols that we can hold, understand, and believe in. But this path of transcendence is ineffable, and humans miss it unless they can enter into the ground of being where God is simply perfect love. The knowledge of God that is gained is found in the experience itself.

In all our transcendent experiences there is no language that is adequate. We have dropped all names and are as God is, beyond mental constructs. We can only talk in metaphors that sound dangerously close to idolatry for those outside of the experience. God cannot be spoken. As we quoted Philip at the beginning of our quest into this mystical text: "One alone is truth and yet she makes the many, and by means of many things, she lovingly teaches this one truth alone to all" (2:3). God can only be known as we come to a deeper knowledge of the many things, for "Reality is one and whole" (5:8).

As we become increasingly spiritually mature, we are made more and more capable of spiritual knowledge. Becoming whole means returning to our source, where we

---

[11] Walshe, *Meister Eckhart Sermons and Treatises, Volume 2*, Sermon 62, 115.

are being transformed into "the Father," and "becoming fatherly," as Philip puts it, or as he then states here, becoming "motherly." The point is, we are becoming as God is. Or, as we have already pointed out, the depths of Love itself is the knowledge and truth we will discover as we become more like God—beings of love, beings of light. The children of God, through grace, maturing into this ineffable evolving divinity.

As we use multiple metaphors and names for God and our transcendent experiences, we are prone to the illusions that Philip warns against, conceptualizing and making sense of that which cannot be understood with our rational mind. God is best disclosed through art, music, poetry, or acts of compassion and love rather than in theology and creeds. We cannot ultimately know God through ideas or theological statements of God. God is neither male nor female, father nor mother, king, judge, warrior, bridegroom, husband, nor is God us! These are simply the naming of our experiences of God. In other words, God is best expressed not as a noun but as a verb. God is love. We can only know God by participation in God, as we are giving birth to God.

Jesus affirmed this way of knowledge when the apostle Philip asked him, "Rabbi, show us Abba God, and that will be enough for us." Jesus replied, "Have I been with you all this time, Philip, and still you don't know me? Whoever has seen me has seen Abba God." Jesus goes on to assure Philip that the words he spoke and the things he did, were not him solely but rather are Abba God, living in him. "Believe me that I am in God and God is in me, or else believe because of the works I do." In other words, God isn't known apart from human manifestation. When God is working in and through us, the world will see and know God, not in any conceptual way whatsoever, but solely as God is undeniably evident in our lives. And then, Jesus says something most profound concerning this: "The truth of the matter is, anyone who has faith in me will do the works I do—and greater works besides" (John 14:8-12).

Symeon the New Theologian speaks of this transcendent experience so beautifully:

> We become members of Christ—and Christ becomes our members, Christ becomes my hand, Christ my miserable foot; and I, unhappy one, am Christ's hand, Christ's foot! I move my hand, and my hand is the whole Christ, since, do not forget it, God is indivisible in God's divinity; I move my foot, and behold it shines like that One! Do not accuse me of blasphemy, but welcome these things and adore Christ who makes you such, since if you so wish you will become a member of Christ, and similarly all our members individually will become members of Christ and Christ our members, and all which is dishonorable in us He will make honorable by adorning it with His divine beauty and His divine glory, since living with God...we shall become gods, no longer seeing the shamefulness of our body at all, but made completely like Christ in our whole body, each member of our body will be the whole Christ; because, becoming many members, He remains unique and indivisible, and each part is He, the whole Christ.[12]

[12] Maloney, *Saint Symeon the New Theologian*, Hymn 15, 217.

GENDER AND GENDERLESS

The human distortions of God's image are reflected in our own self-image. In Philip, the restoration to fullness of being includes the balance of male and female, for they have "not received both the power of the male and the female in equal balance. It is in the bridal chamber where the bride is united with the bridegroom that "this balance is attained" (4:19). What it means to be male or female has been given to us by our various cultures and Philip is claiming that our sexual identities are distorted. However, in transcendent reality a new relationship is found which transcends those separate and immature identities. Jesus said, "When you are able to make two become one, the inside like the outside, and the outside like the inside, the higher like the lower, so that a man is no longer male, and a woman, female, but male and female become a single whole...then you will enter [into the Kingdom of God]."[13]

In our Genesis myth, we're told that Adam was the original human being. But then God created a woman from Adam's rib and duality came into being. Then Adam said, "This at last is bone of my bones and flesh of my flesh; this one shall be called Woman, for out of Man this one was taken" (Genesis 2:23). Philip draws on this story saying,

> If the female had not been separated from the male, she would never have died with the male. Her separation...became the cause and origin of death. It is for this reason that the Anointed One came that he might remedy this condition

[13] The Gospel of Thomas, 22, 17.

> by uniting the masculine and the feminine together again. (4:17)

According to Philip, when Adam and Eve "united outside of the bridal chamber," leaving God out of the experience, they brought duality into our world. No longer was their sexual union based on a spiritual relationship; it was purely physical. The result, Philip says, is that "no one is able to escape being seized by their compulsions" (4:19). The Anointed One, Philip says, rectified this by bringing the masculine and feminine together again "in spiritual union" (4:17). Human sexuality is intended to be a deeply spiritual experience, not just one of flesh. Being spiritual it becomes iconic and leads us to the in-depth experience of uniting the spiritual and physical realms. For God "is creator of all, who is over all and works through all, and is in all" (Ephesians 4:6), bringing about our fullness of being.

We were created in God's image, "male and female" God created us according to Genesis. But God is neither male nor female; God is transcendent to earthly identities. To come to a mature state as God's children we need to also transcend those sexual identities. For the Gospel of Philip this comes through sacred marriage, where the soul is united with God in a new birthing of Christ from within. We then, like Christ, are "married beings" manifesting this new reality, God and humanity are One, heaven and earth are wedded, the spiritual and material worlds are a single whole, bringing a spiritual balance to earth. Jesus said, "Many are standing at the door, but only the single or solitary will enter the place of union."[14]

In both the gospels of Thomas and Mary Magdalene the

---

[14] The Gospel of Thomas, 75, 32,

Apostle Peter expresses a bias against women as incapable of discipleship. In the Gospel of Thomas Peter says, "Mary should leave us, for women are not worthy of this Life." Jesus surprisingly responds, then "I will transform her into a living spirit because any woman changed in this way will enter the Divine Realm."[15] And, of course, this is the transformation that we all, both male or female, must forego. And according to Philip, transcend both sexual identifications.

Peter was expressing his cultural biases and had not yet been transformed in this way. In The Dialogues of Mary Magdalene, likewise, Peter speaks of disbelief in what Mary is reporting Jesus having taught her: "Would the Savior speak these things to a woman in private.... Should we listen to her at all?" Matthew then chastises Peter, "You have always been quick to anger, Peter, and now you are questioning her.... If the Savior considered her worthy, who are you to reject her? He knew her completely and loved her faithfully. We should be ashamed of ourselves! As he taught us, we should be clothed instead with the cloak of true humanity."[16] Indeed, according to Philip, when we are clothed with "the cloak of true humanity" we will transcend what it means to be either male or female.

Defining male or female in spiritual terms goes far beyond our cultural norms. In Philip's understanding we are incomplete beings in our unmarried state. In spiritual marriage Spirit unites and transforms us into whole beings. In transcendent reality, these divine qualities of male and female are only known by their complementarity to one another and have equal value. "It is in the iconic bridal chamber, where the bride is united with the bridegroom that this balance is attained" (4:19). With a new spiritual humanity,

[15] The Gospel of Thomas, 114, 41.
[16] The Dialogues of Mary Magdalene, Dialogue 4, 69.

the genders are now in parity and help define each other. The transcendent identity is neither male nor female but rather a genderless *married being*, a new united expression. Like God, they are spiritually both masculine and feminine, in balance. "When the feminine and the masculine come together in spiritual union within the Bridal Chamber, they are no longer separated" (4:18). Spiritual marriage brings us back to a balance and an equilibrium that makes God one in all things, helping us to become integrated and whole.

At his baptism, Jesus became this new whole human, "my Beloved, my own child," as he was called (Mark 1:11). He became a new fully realized human being, according to Philip, not just male nor female, but a "married being," both the masculine and feminine in parity as God is. Jesus became the Christ, transcending human particularities, and now is the Earth-Child, and is, within themself, masculine and feminine, father and mother, husband and wife, embodying all of humanity with all its extraordinary complexities.

> Indeed, we have been begotten and brought into being by the aid of the Sacred Spirit, and then we were reborn by means of the Anointed One. In both cases it is Spirit who has anointed us, and having thus been reborn, we are now "married beings" (4:6).

Jesus said in the Gospel of Thomas, "When you are able to transform two into one, then you will become a [full] 'Child of Humanity.'"[17] His students said to him,

> "Tell us, who you really are so we may believe in

[17] The Gospel of Thomas, 106, 39.

> you." He said to them, "You have learned to read the face of earth and sky, but you do not yet recognize the one standing in your presence, nor can you make sense of the present moment."[18]

The old polarities have been transcended. "It was in this way that the balance of All was established in Yeshua's heart so that by means of this each of his students might have access to enter into his Rest" (5:2). There is no "rest" until we have come to a balance with the polarities of our lives. To be emptied of self is to be full of God, and to be full of self is to be emptied of God. My part is emptiness of self, God's part is filling what is empty. But this is a marriage, so it is one and the same, there is no separation of actions. It is one action and one in balance, bringing equity in all things. God and I are One. When Jesus said to Philip: "believe me, I am in the Father, and the Father is in me" (John 14:11), he was speaking of spiritual marriage.

In this transcendent state, "I am in God and God is in me" shatters my understanding of myself. Our experience can only tell us, we are a new, whole being, what God is, we are, what God does, we do: one life and one being. The separate self, having died in God, means we have assimilated into God in a transcendent state. We are recreated in this new birthing of Christ, reflecting the divine image. We are capable of both environments, for the two have become one, "the inside like the outside, the outside like the inside," without division.[19] "That we may be One, may God help us. Amen," prayed Meister Eckhart.[20]

---

[18] The Gospel of Thomas, 92, 35.
[19] The Gospel of Thomas, 22, 17.
[20] Walshe, *Meister Eckhart Sermons and Treatises, Volume 1,* Sermon 14, 128.

Philip also applies this transcendent identity to our culture and race. Transcendent humans become a new evolved race, transcending all cultural identities. "It is good to call the offspring who have been chosen by the Sacred Spirit, the 'True Humanity' and 'Sons and Daughters of the Human One'" (4:11). This new humanity is "true human" more fully expressing our divine heritage, more fully and uniquely its own essential being. These new fully realized humans transcend normal human identities of the self: race, sex, and individual.

> Whoever shall receive God outright must have wholly renounced themselves and gone out of themselves: they get straight from God all that God has, as their own just as much as it is God's and our Lady's and all who are in heaven. It belongs equally and as much to them. Those who have gone out of themselves and renounced themselves in equal measure will receive equally, and no less. (Meister Eckhart)[21]

TRANSCENDENT CULTIVATION

When we prepare for the springtime to come, this fulfills the divine imperative for humanity laid out in Genesis:

> Then God said, "Let us make humankind in our image, to be like us. Let them be stewards of the fish in the sea, the birds of the air, the cattle, the wild animals, and everything that crawls on the ground." (Genesis 1:26)

[21] Walshe, *Meister Eckhart Sermons and Treatises, Volume 1*, Sermon 40, 285.

Philip reminds us that the human duty as stewards is to cultivate the earth. Just as the earth is created with the physical elements of minerals, water, air and light, so too, transcendent humans will cultivate with the divine elements of trust, hope love and enlightenment (5:24).

When we reflect God's nature, we will plant the seeds within society that transform humanity and bring the earth into greater balance and beauty. Without this cultivation the earth will never evolve into its highest potential. Trust, hope, love, and enlightenment are the component elements of the earth-body that gives it spiritual health and vitality; and the medicines that will heal its wounds. This amelioration is essential for earth's transcendence, otherwise it will decline spiritually, atrophy, and die. This becomes more urgent every day that passes. We'll never heal until we can trust, and we'll never trust until we have hope for our future. We can never have hope for our future until we can see the many things through the eyes of love, an enlightenment that is the result of our consummate marriage to God.

Element of Trust [pistis]

Trust is a core component of spiritual nurturance. The "one who has begun to trust the truth is fully alive" (5:16). Without trust in the goodness of creation, there is a fear of its wildness and freedom and of all that is outside human control. To trust the Spirit within creation means we set creation free to be wild, which also is allowing ourselves to be vulnerable and open to the unknown—to be visionary, creative, imaginative, and unpredictable, apart from our own needs to control and protect, presenting a clean canvas for God's handiwork.

To trust God means we believe in the trustworthiness of the Creator, which most humans have not learned to do.

Trusting in our Creator's worthiness and love is to put trust in our own growth and development beyond our control or expectations. We must learn to live within the limitations of our human experience, while being open to and accepting this as the pathway to transcendence. Trust allows us to detach from self-control and become vulnerable and anticipatory, putting faith in the Spirit's work within us. Cultivating trust means loving and supporting others as they too learn to live in trust and vulnerability.

The bottom line is that God is good and the earth is our "garden of paradise" where we can thrive, and we must seed the world with this element! This will set it free to fulfill God's dream for the earth.

> I give praise to your holy Nature, Beloved, for you have made my nature a sanctuary for your hiddenness and a tabernacle for your mysteries, a place where you can dwell, and a holy temple for your Divinity, namely, for the One who holds the scepter of your reign, who governs all you have brought into being, the glorious Tabernacle of your eternal Being, the source of renewal for the ranks of fire which minister to you, the Way to knowledge of you, the Door to the vision of you, the summation of your power and great wisdom. (Isaac the Syrian)[22]

Element of Hope [elpis]

Hope is akin to trust in that it is based on faith and love. Fear is the predominant human condition that blocks our trust in God's providence. Fear has brought the world to its

[22] Isaac the Syrian, as quoted in Alfeyev, *The Spiritual World of Saint Isaac the Syrian*, 57.

present disordered condition and has destroyed hope in its future. Restoring hope for the earth is part of the antidote to endemic fear. Hope is a metaphysical principle in that the universe has spiritual potentialities awaiting realization. Evolution is a hopeful and wild enterprise, and evidence of the Creator's confidence. All things, according to Philip, arise through some form of incarnation and thus are aspects of God. To bring this knowledge into our consciousness is to open our hearts in aspiration. Hope holds a necessary vision for the possibilities of reaching our human potential. And without hope, we're diminished and held back by fear.

Hope is the necessary quality that allows creation to flourish, causing countless birds and butterflies, animals, and humans to take dangerous migration journeys. Hope causes plants to evolve and adapt to change. Hope has driven human immigration throughout the world. Hope is a blank canvass, an empty page, and an uncarved stone or piece of wood. Hope is medicine for despair and futility. Hope is the source of marriages and the birth of new children. Nature teaches us hope through all the cycles and seasons: spring, summer, autumn, and winter. Without hope our world would not have persevered in facing the immense challenges and threats to life.

Hope frees us to imagine the goodness of all things, trusting that we were made for this earthly experience, with its gamut of joys and sorrows. Hope believes in the goodness of God that love will prevail over evil. Hope means that I embrace not only those whom I love, but eventually all humankind.

If my hope is for my own transcendence, or becoming more attuned to the image of God, then I must realize how I cannot find my own fullness apart from the many things. We are bound to one another and to the whole earth, and our future is dependent upon each other's welfare. If the reign of God is my hope for the earth, then it means a transformation so radical as to envision "a new heaven and a new earth" as we presently know it. Spiritual hope even transcends death. Hope trusts in the evolutionary forces within the earth and God's goodness and love for all creation.

Element of Love (agape)

Love is foundational to hope for it frees the heart of its restrictions, opening it to new and unknown possibilities. Hope transcends fear by raising our spiritual sight. Hope awakens the transcendent soul to the imaginal realm where the impossible becomes possible and where the reign of God is actualized. It is a divine imperative without which the universe wouldn't have come into being. Hope sees good in the midst of evil, light in the darkness, and the perfect in imperfection. It is love's handmaiden in our journey into the mysterious unknown.

Love is the greatest creative force in the universe and the power that causes us to be drawn to another in love and tenderness, and ultimately to God and self-transcendence. Love opens our hearts where we discover our essential selves in God. Our first and immature love is the very human experience of relationships with family, spouses, and friends. As we come into spiritual maturity, we're drawn into an experience of God through the power of love. This transcendent love, according to Philip, lifts our consciousness to its higher realms, freeing us for greater self-transcendence. For Philip, the evidence of love is found in service to the world. We are made to love in order to give (3:32). This is the highest expression of our unity with God. Isaac the Syrian speaks of it too: "Love that arises from within us is like a small lamp fed by oil, and thus its light is sustained.... But love that has

God as its cause is like a spring gushing forth, and its streams are never cut off, for God alone is the source of love, and its substance is inexhaustible."[23]

Human love naturally reaches its limits in the familial and sexual, but in our love of God we are drawn into unity with all being, our love for all things flowing from the love of God. In following Jesus our love must transcend that of family and kin.[24] In transcendent love there is no longer any self-centeredness or any place for my separate ego. This love, expressed through self-giving is the medicine that will heal humanity for "love covers a multitude of sins," says Philip (3:31). Spiritual marriage, Philip says, "makes me a slave of love." This gift enlarges my capacity for greater love, even reaching beyond my comprehension. Love opens our spiritual intellect to its highest potential. Ultimately, my love of God and love of earth are one because God is One, and unity with God makes us transcendent lovers.

Human love, based as it is on self-concerns and needs is naturally transactional, giving in order to get what we want. Spiritual love, however, called *agape* in the New Testament Greek, is the gift of unity and transcends normal human self-interests. *Agape*-love is a spiritual gift that raises the consciousness of the many things to its greatest heights.[25] Only through this love do we, at last, fully become the Christ and evidence the face of God.

Element of Enlightenment [gnosis]

Humanity's greatest natural evolutionary achievement is its acumen and intelligence. And the opening to human

---

[23] Isaac the Syrian, *Ascetical Homilies*, Homily 31, 115.

[24] The Gospel of Thomas, 101, 38.

[25] I often call *agape*-love "transcendent love," or "conscious love" in that it transcends the bounds of normal human love through our conscious choice to become self-giving lovers as God is.

transcendence lies through the intellect. Transcending normal human knowledge is the extraordinary experience of enlightenment.

Jesus, at his baptism, came into enlightenment, according to Philip, as witnessed by John the Baptizer. Conventional human intelligence is limited to mental cognition and reasoning. This level of consciousness is a mark of higher evolutionary achievement for the many things, but can be an impediment to greater enlightenment, which can only happen when we're freed from the constraints of our minds. Our minds are limited to the lens of our senses and cultural norms. But a higher intellect is experienced when the heart is awakened through contemplation to intuitive knowing.

For many people, there's an attempt to limit knowledge to the realm of the empirical, observable by the senses. But to deny that there is any knowledge beyond the rational is to be ignorant of the transcendent, which is not wholly objectifiable. There is a path to higher intelligence and it lies by way of the heart. The heart being the holiest of holy places is the meeting place between the Spirit and the soul. It is here that we come to a unity of being at last. In other words, we can only know spiritual knowledge by becoming spiritually whole.

Humanity was made to have this knowledge of God, and it is our next evolutionary threshold. But few have attained it.

This knowledge is found through a process of not knowing. It requires us to be detached from our mental limitations and awakened to the heart's intuitive expansive knowing. This higher intellect can be gained through *agape*-love. Those who are spiritually married, according to Philip "have gained wisdom from truth...and having transcended their state in the world, are free" from their mental constraints and total self-interests (3:29). This is a gift for the evolution of the earth, and it is possible for humanity if it's willing to turn from self-obsessions and dependence on mental acuity as the sole path to knowledge, and open its heart to all-inclusive being.

Enlightenment is experienced as insight which comes as direct knowledge, rather than information mediated from outside sources or rational processes. This greater level of consciousness is universal in that it is connected to and accessed through spirit. Philip says, "It is not possible for a person to see the higher realities of existence unless that person has become as real as they are." It then becomes the natural process of intuitive insight; natural because "what [we] see from beyond comes because [we] are transcending [consciously] towards them" (3:4).

These four elements of trust, hope, love, and enlightenment are spiritual forces that will change the evolutionary trajectory of the earth. Jesus, Philip says, used his powers "to bring everything in existence under cultivation, and for this reason whatever there is whether for good or ill, on the right hand or on the left, exists" (5:27). Our earthly experience is meant to bring us to a spiritual cultivation. The cultivation of the earth is the awakening of the divine nature of the many things. All things are to be brought to their fruition and wholeness through a spiritual marriage. "Our soil is the heart where trust takes root. Hope is the water through which we are nourished. Love is the wind by which we grow, and enlightenment is the Light which causes us to ripen" (5:32).

EARTH-CENTERED SPIRITUALITY

This spiritual cultivation means a radical shift in our relationships. Rather than seeing the world through a human lens perspective, we shift to an earth-centered spirituality where the many things are valued equally with the human. As we sow these elements into our world, and our relationship to the earth is transformed, we will set it free to heal of its own relationship to Spirit.

When neglected, the earth remains out of balance, and is "devouring itself"' (5:9). To shirk our responsibility to it is to sin not only against our Creator but against the whole universe to which we are kin. Humans are given a primary role in creation's evolution! Without spiritual cultivation the earth is imperiled. And without spiritual transformation humans cannot cultivate the earth. It is our perceived separation from nature that is at the root of our malady. To see nature as separate and lesser than us is to desecrate and misuse it out of ignorance. But when our consciousness is raised, we have a role to play. "In love will the whole course of the governance of creation be finally comprised," said Isaac the Syrian.[26] And then there's Philip:

> So now in this way [the Anointed One] comes to receive back what he has always loved—releasing all who were held captive by thieves of the soul, redeeming everything in the cosmos, both good and evil. (5:4)

St. Paul said something similar: "Through Christ, the world was fully reconciled again to God, who didn't hold our transgressions against us, but instead entrusted us with this message of reconciliation. This makes us Christ's ambassadors, as though God were making the appeal directly through us" (1 Corinthians 5:19-20).

---

[26] Brock, *The Wisdom of Saint Isaac the Syrian*, 31.

Our blindness and distance are our primary failings. "But the one who has begun to know the truth is fully alive" (5:16). Until enlightenment, we're blinded and unconscious of spiritual realities. Philip warns against trying to come to truth through intellect alone (2:1). Our intellect has kept us ignorant of higher knowledge, skimming only on the surface of life. We cannot be conscious of that of which we are unconscious—and we're especially unconscious of the presence of God "in whom we live, move and have our being" (Acts 17:28). Our ignorance and hubris veil a deeper perception of the essential nature and purpose of all things. Meister Eckhart put it this way:

> The humble person and God are one.... What God performs the humble person performs, and what God is, that person is: one life and one being. That is why our dear Lord said, "Learn from me, who am gentle and humble-hearted."[27]

This consciousness was already present in the native peoples who were closer to and in balance with the world they inhabited. Their language often expressed these truths, but the invaders couldn't hear it since they weren't listening! They were blinded by greed and hubris. They could not see the spiritual condition of the societies they encountered. For present day humans, this means humbling ourselves and changing our language to express more clearly what a new relationship with the natural world entails. We must shift our language to personhood in relationship to the natural world, for it too embodies the divine image and is reflecting in its essential being the beauty, truth and goodness of God.

---

[27] Walshe, *Meister Eckhart Sermons and Treatises, Volume 2*, Sermon 50, 45.

We need to be humble enough to begin speaking of our kinship with plants, animals, and minerals, acknowledging their co-equal relationship and value to our own. The many things are persons as much as we are, because the Spirit indwells them. As our consciousness grows, we will also come to recognize the earth's elements as holy with God's presence: water, air, minerals and fire, all expressing God's unique qualities, and like ourselves, incarnated by the Spirit and therefore our relations. Philip says:

> When that which is from above comes into manifestation it is commonly thought to be from below. When something is hidden or unmanifest it is often said to be from above. It is important, therefore, that the interior and the exterior exist together beyond all externals. (3:11)

To see the earth as an incarnate being, "whose glory gives beauty to everything," (2:18) is to perceive its essential nature. Philip says that "Living water is itself a being" (2:19), as are all the elements of the earth as seen from the divine perspective. It is only our limited sight that prevents us from seeing the holy nature of the many things.

But our practice of meditating upon God's presence with us changes and transforms our perspective of nature herself. "Remembering God" opens us to a communion with all things also at one with this divine energy. When this sight is gained, we will know ourselves in deep kinship. And the objectification of nature by us will end. Jesus affirmed this when he said, "Whoever knows the cosmos discovers the body, but the cosmos does not deserve the one who makes that discovery."[28]

---

[28] The Gospel of Thomas, 80, 33.

FINAL NOTE

RENDING THE VEIL

We have little history or writings to tell us how this second-century sect of Christians practiced their faith. We know that they were considered a mainstream sect. And we can deduce what their practices were by what is written and taught in the Gospel of Philip.

For these early Jewish-Christian mystics, the rites of the church were of paramount importance and a primary focus. They believed that Jesus left an internal path in which we can each find our fullness of being. But when much of the church, in becoming a "Christian" sect, focused too exclusively on these external rites and beliefs, the disciples of Philip's Gospel sought "higher realities of existence" (3:4) by rending the veil of the external icons—where transcendent knowledge was found.

For us today, their insights should also affect our Christian religious traditions and practices, balancing the exoteric forms of worship with the esoteric teachings and practices. For many today, religious observance is primarily centered on external beliefs and practices, and the Christian rites are ends in themselves. But following Jesus into this esoteric journey we must reframe what it means to be his followers. Rather than holding to a rigid set of beliefs, we now follow Christ based on his primary teachings on esoteric practices (3:11). As Jesus said in the Gospel of Thomas:

"Whoever drinks what flows from my mouth will come to be as I am."[1]

While the Imperial Church demands we accept a theology about Jesus and a mythology of his life, Philip instead invites us into Jesus' esoteric teachings and practices which start with the heart's engagement. Philip's starting point is never theology or mythology, but a prayerful encounter with the living Christ found through contemplative prayer. For Philip, the active agent of transformation is transcendent love, experienced in communion. As we move away from a self-focused life to one of conscious love, we're taking on the divine attributes of self-giving love—*agape*-love.

Jesus summed up his path to a transformation of humanity when he said it is all contained in "loving one's neighbor as oneself." And as Philip teaches, "everything rises through some form of incarnation, for everything is held there in its very heart" (2:26). We are all one in being, and love binds us together.

In the Gospel of Mary Magdalene, Mary tells of a vision she had of Jesus, and the teachings she received:

> I said to him: "Master, in this moment of vision what sees you? Is it the soul or the spirit?" And he answered me, "It is neither soul nor spirit that sees, but the eye of the heart which is between the two that perceives the vision."[2]

Philip is inviting us inside, to discover the eyes and ears of our hearts where a higher path to knowledge of God can be found. Today's Christian church needs to "bring interiority

[1] The Gospel of Thomas, 108, 39.
[2] The Dialogues of Mary Magdalene, Dialogue 2, 67.

into the outer world" if it is to be the dynamic emissary of Jesus it purports to be (3:13).

During the fourth century, Church councils formulated creeds and myths upon which to base an orthodoxy of Christian faith. This shut down a deeper searching for the living word of God, still being spoken today. Much of the Church believes that God is no longer speaking, since he spoke in Jesus and ended further revelation. But this is erroneous, and the Imperial Church needs to abandon staid belief as the starting point and return to a new trust in the Holy Spirit, who continues to lead us into ongoing truth (cf. John 16:13). Trusting in the dynamic work of God in our lives is primary to being a disciple of Jesus Christ and his mission on earth.

Jesus once asked his followers why they followed him out into the wilderness:

> To see a reed blown about by the wind? A man dressed in soft raiment like your rulers and the powerful? Yes, indeed they are clothed in fine, luxurious garments, but what they lack is the ability to discern truth.[3]

What he offers his followers is "the ability to discern truth." He's given us of his own spirit to lead and guide and enlighten us. If Christians are to follow Jesus, they must find that living word active and accessible within them.

The very term "Church" points "away from reality into illusion" according to Philip (2:1). From the exoteric viewpoint, the Church might erroneously be understood as an institution, or buildings, or an earthly kingdom of God. But

[3] The Gospel of Thomas, 78, 33.

the Church, in Philip's understanding, is those who are at one with God and are thus temples of God, not made with hands nor of human origin. These are those Christ "took inside" (3:13) into the bridal chamber and are now birthing the Christ into our world; living and vibrant temples of God, who have been "brought forth into eternal reality" (5:4).

Imperial Christianity has often distorted the meaning of the icons, the Christian mysteries (the rites of the Church), not seeing their unfathomable depths, confusing their message and purpose. This blindness has thwarted many from their God-given gift of sacred marriage where truth is discovered. When religion has lost its dynamic message, its mission—which is primarily to assist individuals in finding their path to transcendence—is lost, as well. Without this transcendent path we are kept, unfortunately, at the breast of our mother our whole lives, dependent on Mother Church.

The goal of all moral formation and the rites of the Church are to assist seekers in coming into a mature state of sovereignty (3:26).[4] These rites, rituals, and teachings are meant to channel our spiritual energies, assisting each person in the process of transformation and deliverance from ignorance. Transformation means a whole change in our understanding of what it means to be a human being, from merely animal nature to a Christ-being, at one with God, having divine qualities. Jesus said, "When you are able to transform two into one, then you will become a 'Son of Humanity.'"[5] When we become one with God as Jesus was,

[4] "Yeshua said, 'If you are searching, you must not stop until you find. When you find, however, you will become troubled. Your confusion will give way to wonder. In wonder you will reign over all things. Your sovereignty will be your rest.'" (The Gospel of Thomas, 2)

[5] The Gospel of Thomas, 106, 39.

then the Church will have fulfilled its mission as Christ's agent in the world.

The mysteries of Christianity are not ends in themselves, but teachings meant to lead us to their deeper and innermost knowledge; a truer understanding of the many things which are points of intersection between creation and its Creator. Without transcendent realities, the rites of the Church are dead. Jesus spoke about religion in his own time:

> Your scholars and religious leaders have taken the keys of knowledge and locked them away. They have not used them to enter in, nor have they allowed those desiring it to do so. You, therefore, must be as subtle as serpents and as guileless as doves.[6]

Primary to the Gospel of Philip is humanity's intrinsic sacredness, which has "a natural kinship to that which is truly good" (5:13). For these followers of Christ, humanity was essentially righteous, being children of God, and meant to go on to maturity and become fully realized (3:26).

TRANSCENDENTAL PERCEPTION

In the Gospel of Mary Magdalene, Jesus is quoted saying:

> Sin as such does not exist. You only bring it into manifestation when you act in ways that are adulterous in nature. It is for this very reason that the Good has come among you pursuing

[6] The Gospel of Thomas, 39, 21.

> its own essence within nature in order to unite everything with its origin.[7]

If we could see as God sees, "then nothing in this world would be considered evil, nor would we see ourselves merely as temporal creatures," says Philip (2:1). Nothing in creation is evil for all things are created good. It is, however, within the human potential not only to bring our innate goodness into our world, but evil as well.

> Yeshua says.... Good people bring goodness out of a storehouse of inner treasure, and evil ones bring wickedness out of the repository of evil collected in the heart. It is from there that they speak. For from the heart's overflow evil enters the world. (The Gospel of Thomas)[8]

This is why human consciousness is so consequential. Separated from our Creator, humans have turned away from God. All things are created by love and are thus intrinsically beautiful, true, and good, but we have the freedom to choose our own path, including that which is opposed to the divine will. Philip's whole intention was to bring us to wholeness of being: "If truth is fully revealed, even [evil persons] can be brought to perfection" (4:1).

When Christians return to Jesus' inner path of transcendent knowledge, it is consonant with coming into unity with God. This means returning to a place of humility and openness, acknowledging that we only have this present moment to free God to be God in and through us. God must be unfettered from all our creeds and theologies and undefined in

[7] The Dialogues of Mary Magdalene, Dialogue 1, 65.
[8] The Gospel of Thomas, 45, 22.

order to be freed to be the God of the present, active here and now. We must come to an unknowing if we are to come to a present knowledge of God. God will be—not what we think or want God to be—but simply as God is, in this present moment, in these particular circumstances. "There is no other place transcendent to this" (3:11).

Our set of old beliefs and doctrines could thwart this immanent experience. Holding to our concepts of God blinds us to the God present at this moment. This openness to the divine presence will be the catalyst to bring Christ into our world in our own day through our lives.

Unfortunately, the Imperial Church teaches that humans are intrinsically evil, having inherited a sinful nature from Adam's fall. As a result, they teach that it was necessary that Jesus died as an atonement. From this point of view, by accepting this gift of grace we are granted salvation in the world to come. But this takes away our innate human agency and the necessary transformation of being. This distorted teaching is an aberration of the gospel of Jesus Christ and has eroded true discipleship, which requires I must turn my back on my own self in order to find my true self. To see oneself, and others, as evil and rejected by God is to distort our understanding of God and blind us to the knowledge of our own value, purpose, and meaning. Consequently, most of us "are not able to look upon the icon of our own being"[9] in self-knowledge and are thus on a path of self-destruction.

Christians also often speak of God as outside our world, in a heavenly place, judging and controlling things. Spirituality for too many is simply holding to a set of beliefs and myths, believing that if they please God they will be blessed and if they displease God they will be cursed. The

[9] The Gospel of Thomas, 84, 34.

Church's mission is, they believe, evangelism, i.e. convincing others of these exclusive beliefs. This, too, is a distortion of Jesus' teachings.

Perhaps unintentionally, the Church authorities have tended to "make us slaves to themselves through time" (5:13), keeping us dependent and thus in a lower state of consciousness. But Jesus said to his friends, "Cursed are your religious leaders for they are like dogs sleeping in the feed bin. They do not eat nor do they allow the cattle to eat."[10] The antidote, according to Philip, is that "divine power has been granted humanity," in order to become fully realized human beings, finding our freedom in transcendence (5:13). "Love," Philip says, "will uplift and free us" (3:29). And the Church must carry this message to humanity.

Jesus has taught us to follow him in the "way of the cross," becoming humble and meek, turning away from a self-focused life, to know God as our parent at a lower level of knowledge, and to experience God as our lover in a higher conscious state. And yet there's a higher state, when we're able to look upon Jesus and "see ourselves" it will "enable us his students also to become great" (3:10). "To see one's true self," Philip says, "it is necessary to be immersed in both—the light as well as the water" (3:5), wedding the higher and lower realms.

Jesus came, according to Philip, to awaken humanity to its transcendence, uniting the virgin soul with its ground of being. "I came that you might have life, and have it to the full," Jesus said (John 10:10). So if the Church is to become relevant in this moment, it must help humanity *rend the veil* in order to see from the inside. And to see oneself from

[10] The Gospel of Thomas, 102, 38.

this viewpoint. In the tenth century, Symeon the New Theologian described his own experience of this:

> Listen, if you wish, to these more mystical secrets! When this fire burns brightly, and it chases away the swarm of passions and purifies the interior of your soul, then it mingles with it without merging with it and it unites with it in an unspeakable manner, its essence with the essence of the soul, absolutely in a total way, and little by little it illumines the soul. It sets it on fire and makes it light, and—how to express it I am unable—the two become one, the soul is with the Creator and the Creator is in the soul; alone, totally, with the soul alone, He who holds the whole creation in His own hand. Do not doubt it, this One, completely one with the Father and the Spirit, takes up a place in a single soul and completely surrounds the soul, taking it wholly within Gods own Self. Think of, look at, meditate on these things![11]

FULLY REALIZED HUMANITY

When the Church comes to understand its true mission, it will, through its teachings, open the path of transcendence to all people, where they will ultimately transcend religion itself as they experience union with God. The goal and purpose of religion having been achieved.

Philip beautifully states that we are presently in the garden of paradise, though we may be unaware of this truth.

[11] Maloney, *Saint Symeon the New Theologian*, Hymn 30, 331.

This isn't some mythological realm; God has created the environment in which we can thrive and evolve and has given us authority over creation (5:29). But human ignorance and unconsciousness destroys the reign of God, and the paradise into which we have been born. Many of us, ignorant of our spiritual relationship to this paradisical garden, are destroying our God-created utopia. In this earthly garden, designed by our creator, we are meant to evolve and awaken to our highest potential, even becoming co-creators in this amazing enterprise, at one with God seeding the earth with divine elements!

The Gospel of Philip says: "God created the garden of paradise and humankind dwelt there, but God's desires were not in their hearts" (5:18). This is a heartbreaking analysis of our human condition.

But when our spiritual eyes are opened, "it has already become the Great Age of the Eternal Now whose fullness is no longer hidden" (4:15). The earth, indeed, is full of God's glory for the creation is seen for what it truly is, Godself. "There is one God and Creator of all, who is over all, who works through all and is within all," Paul says so clearly in his more mystical writings (Ephesians 4:5). All things are reflecting God's beauty, goodness, and truth, and are being nurtured and sustained by the overflowing life of God.

When at last we come to realize that this world in which we live embodies the only God we know, we will recognize that it is here, in this place, that God dwells. It is here where we live and move and have our being that we come to a knowledge of truth already ours. It is only here on this earthly plane that our souls discover the reality of love. It is here that we commune with God in God's garden. It is here where we learn to love and be loved. And "if one does not receive it [here] there is nowhere else to receive it" (4:15).

As we commune with God, we will increasingly become more and more like God. Philip says, "The Sacred Spirit becomes visible when descending towards the material plane, and invisible when ascending towards transcendent realities" (2:7). In other words, we cannot perceive God except through this incarnational experience, in this physical body—not in a conceptual way whatsoever. God is always evidenced through relationships. As we are assimilating into God, we are also birthing God through outpourings of creativity, imagination, love, and compassion.

The bounty of God's goodness cannot be expressed in reality without our conscious participation. Without our actions, now grounded in Spirit, God's beauty, goodness, and perfection cannot be known and seen in plenitude. As we give birth to the Christ, through our union with God, our world will experience God present here and now. God is made real to the world through our authenticity of being.

A fully realized human being is one who has found fulfillment and unity with the divine essence. Now, a living temple of God, this fully realized person has come into their sovereignty and fullness. As we come into this fulfilled state, we see more clearly. This is what Philip means when it says "we too are also called 'the Christ' just as Yeshua was" (2:12). Meister Eckhart echoed this:

> Whoever has God thus essentially, takes God divinely, and for them God shines forth in all things, for all things taste divinely to them, and God's image appears to them from out of all things. God flashes forth in them always and they bear the imprint of their beloved, present God.[12]

[12] Walshe, *Meister Eckhart Sermons and Treatises, Volume 3*, The Talks of Instruction, 18.

In another passage, Philip says "that through the image of the Bridal Chamber...one is brought into the truth of the restoration of all things...[for] they have also become 'the Christ,' the Anointed One" (2:8). Here is Philip's vision that "all things" participate in the one incarnation and are destined to "lovingly teach this one truth to all" (2:3). The many things revealing God in transcendent love. Isaac the Syrian speaks to this:

> Love is the wine which makes glad the heart of humanity. Blessed is the one who partakes of this wine! Licentious people have drunk this wine and become chaste; sinners have drunk it and have forgotten the pathways of stumbling; drunkards have drunk this wine, and become sober; the rich have drunk it and desired poverty; the poor have drunk it and been enriched with hope; the sick have drunk it and become strong; the unlearned have taken it and become wise.[13]

Love has drawn us to this mystical endeavor. And now the Lover must assimilate into newness of being because in unity of being there is no "other." It is no longer love calling us to the work but love having become itself—that which is calling us and that which is answering having become one in a new manifestation of being.

"Such beings," Philip concludes, "have already received the Truth through the image of the icons and whether they leave this world or act within it in a public way, it has already become for them the Great Age of the Eternal Now whose

[13] Alfeyev, *The Wisdom of Isaac the Syrian*, 255.

fullness is no longer hidden by the darkness of night but has burst forth revealing itself to them" (4:15). This is the Gospel that Jesus taught when he said, "the Reign of God is here amongst us" (Luke 17:21). He knew that the medicine for the world's ills was reuniting creation to its ground of being. "The Father's realm is spreading out across the face of the earth, and humanity is not able to perceive it."[14] And this is why our work is so essential, as Paul explained: "God's will was to make known the priceless Glory which this mystery brings to the nations—the mystery of Christ in you, the hope of glory. This is the Christ we proclaim" (Colossians 1:27-28).

These first Christian mystics carried this essential message of the Gospel of Philip into the world through the fourth century, when it was buried. It has now been resurrected as a message to save humanity and heal the earth.

[14] The Gospel of Thomas, 113, 41.

Ward J. Bauman was ordained an Episcopal priest in 1989 and served parishes in the Bay Area of California for more than a decade, becoming a popular retreat leader in areas of Christian mysticism as well. In 2002, he moved to Minnesota to run The Episcopal House of Prayer, a retreat and conference center on the grounds of St. John's Benedictine Abbey in Collegeville. He invited master teachers to join him in teaching Christian mysticism there as they began the Wisdom Schools, bringing together groups seeking deeper and practical teachings on human spirituality. It was then that Ward first began to teach from the Gospel of Philip and to introduce it to a wider audience. He coauthored with Lynn Bauman and Cynthia Bourgeault *The Luminous Gospels: Thomas, Mary Magdalene, and Philip*. He lives in Minneapolis.

We are

Monkfish Book Publishing

...an independent press publishing spiritual and literary books from a diverse range of perspectives. Genres include memoirs, wisdom literature, fiction, and scholarly works of thought. Monkfish books appeal to the seasoned or novice seeker as well as to the general public looking for reliable sources on spirituality. The readers we had in mind when we began Monkfish in 2002 were devoted spiritual seekers, the type whose passion for the spiritual quest would lead them to read across a dazzling array of traditions: Buddhist, Hindu, Jewish, Christian, Muslim, Native American and more. It has always been our intent to publish works of spiritual authenticity for the general public as well as the specialist and scholar.

Our books are available from booksellers everywhere.

Use this QR code to see recently published books:

Use this one to sign-up for our monthly newsletter:

www.ingramcontent.com/pod-product-compliance
Lightning Source LLC
Jackson TN
JSHW021219090326
98767JS00001B/1

* 9 7 8 1 9 6 6 6 0 8 2 3 3 *